Des Pawson's
Knot Craft

D1319925

Des Pawson's
Knot Craft

*The book that makes all
other knot books work*

Des Pawson
Illustrated by Ann Norman

Paradise Cay Publications, Inc.
P. O. Box 29, Arcata, CA 95518-0029
USA

This book is dedicated to those forgotten and anonymous sailors, riggers, sailmakers, fendermakers and other workers in rope who passed their knowledge on to the next generation so these skills can be with us today. Thank you.

ISBN 939837633

Edited by Linda Scantlebury, www.we-edit.com

Note: While all reasonable care has been taken in the publication of this book, the author and publisher take no responsibility for the use of the methods or products described in the book.

Published by Paradise Cay Publications, Inc.
P. O. Box 29
Arcata, CA 95518-0029
800-736-4509
707-822-9163 Fax
paracay@humboldt1.com
www.paracay.com

Contents

Publisher's Note

Knot Craft was originally published by Adlard Coles in the United Kingdom. Before publication in the United States, the text was edited to conform it to the American idiom. The most important and extensive change was the conversion of metric to inch measurements. Conversion is approximate to the nearest ⅛". This should not cause any problems when using the book.

Introduction

Many books have been published on how to tie practical knots, and a lesser number on decorative knotting, but while the latter may show how to make a fancy knot, they don't give much help in putting the knots together to make an object, be it key fob, fender, bellrope, mat or lanyard. Sometimes there may be an illustration of a finished item for inspiration or even a couple of projects, but rarely is there a step-by-step breakdown, complete with the exact size and lengths of materials required and with full tying instructions: the complete recipe for the very thing you want to make. Here, I hope, is the book that does just that.

Not having enough cordage is a constant risk. You try remembering how much line went into an item you have made in the past, but it is soon forgotten and you are back to guessing, hoping that you have guessed correctly or with a bit to spare. Then comes the day when you have a length of good old rope and you want to make a mat with it; the length is tight--if only you knew the exact amount needed. Or you have 20 feet of super-fine tarred ⅛" twine left. Will this be enough for that bell rope you wanted to make as a special gift, or having started will it be too short and the 20 feet wasted? The wasting of rope, new or old, is something that any owner, skipper, mate, bosun or craftsman abhors. Cordage is a precious material to be valued, treasured, and conserved.

After many years of guesswork and the occasional note in the margins of my knotting books, I belatedly started to keep a Recipe Book in 1977. This told me the finished size of the item I had made, what material I had used, and how much was needed to make it. I added the special little tricks and hints that helped the item to fall right and to be finished neatly. I sketched the special knot that was needed or noted the book that had this information. I have to confess that not everything got recorded, but over the years I have built up a great body of information.

In this book I share with you a selection of the designs from that Recipe Book. When demonstrating I am often asked how to make the various things that I have around me, so here are the basic designs, their sizes, and which knots and sennits are used to make them. I give you a list of materials and their lengths and sizes, and I have made the lengths very slightly generous because all materials vary in the way they make up, and each craftsman's knotting tension differs. You may well wish to adjust the material lengths to suit yourself and your favorite cordage. The stated materials and knots will make what I describe, but it is always possible to make items using bigger or smaller line. It can help to keep a record of any variations, because the more information you have the better your guesses will be in the future.

As this book is a "recipe book" rather than a how-to-tie-knots book (there is a good list of these at the end of this book), I have simply named the knots and sennits that go to make up each item. This in itself can lead to a degree of misunderstanding, as many knots have more than one name, so in most cases there is a simple aide-memoire for the more specialized knots or techniques. Rather than repeating them every time they crop up in a design, you will be referred to the page with the illustration.

These are my designs, the knots put together in the way I prefer, but there is no reason why you should not mix and match to create your own designs. Cordage is a versatile medium, and a joy to use for creating all sorts of things.

The aim of this book is to give you the confidence to start making things with knots; it is the book that will make other knot books work for you.

HAPPY KNOTTING.

Des Pawson

Acknowledgments

My special thanks to Ann Norman, who has turned all my scribbles and bits of rope into such clear diagrams and enhanced the book with her special illustrations. The book would be nothing without them. She never once complained at my request for any modifications or tweakings, being always happy to get things right. Any error that may be found is my responsibility.

Some Tips of the Trade

During my years of working with rope I have come across pieces of information, special solutions, tools and techniques from many sources that have in some way been of significant help or interest, and I would like to pass on as many of these as I can.

Tools

Heaving mallet

This sadly neglected tool is a great help in pulling tight stubborn strands in a large rope splice, for tightening seizings, and anywhere else that an extra bit of pull is needed. It works best with a heaving board to pull/heave against.

Heaver

When I was in Mariehamn, the rigger on the *Pommern* known as "Little Brother" showed me a heaver made from a piece of metal pipe with a slot at one end and holes at the other. The strand, or line, is put in the slot and a spike put through the hole; the tool is then turned like a key to tighten the strand or line.

Marlinespike

Look for a good long taper on your marlinespike. I prefer a rounded, flattened point. As with all tools it is rare that a brand new tool is perfect, so it is well worth the trouble to

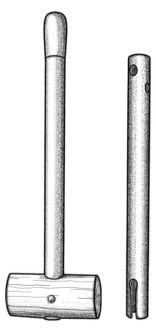

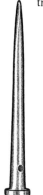

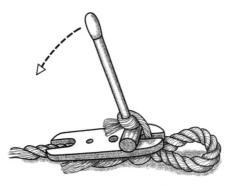

Heaving board (with mallet)

smooth and adjust the shape to your own ideal.

If you are going to use your marlinespike aloft, then ensure there is a hole so that you can fit a lanyard.

Swedish fid

The tool that makes a living for me is the Swedish fid, so called because the original was patented by a Swede, A. J. Svenson, in 1953. It comes in a number of sizes. After any sharp edges have been smoothed and the end nicely rounded, it is a far better tool for most work than the traditional wooden fid. When it is tucked into the rope or knot, it forms a channel for a strand to pass along and the groove means that a better grip is obtained when working a knot tight with its tip.

Looking after wooden fids

Fids are really only stretching tools; they are not levers. Many a wooden fid has had its end broken because it has been used to lever open strands. If there is a need to lever, use a steel marline spike to open out the strand before pushing the fid well in, and use a bit of tallow to ease the passage of the tool.

Little marlinespikes

These can be made from a 6-inch nail with a sharpened end and a Turk's head round its head. A small sharpened metal meat skewer has been in my ditty bag since I was a boy. A screwdriver can also be shaped up for a makeshift marlinespike.

Left to right: Heaving mallet, Heaver, Fid, Marlinespike, Swedish fid, Little marlinespike, Loop tool

6-inch nails

These are also good for pegging out such items as bowsprit nets and scramble nets on the lawn.

Loop tools

I have made up loop tools with various lengths and gauges of bent piano wire, which can be obtained from model shops. I have found that the wire center from morse cable controls will also work. Short loop tools are good for pulling the ends through on small button knots, while long tools will be of help for splicing braid on braid line and for pulling through the lashing strands when making up the cores for a button fender.

Serving stick

A very good replacement for a serving mallet or serving board is a narrow piece of wood in which a series of holes is drilled. The line is threaded through the holes to give the required tension and the serving applied in the normal manner. A very short serving stick will enable you to serve quite small eyes.

Knives

There is much debate about what makes a good knife and what makes a good blade (will it keep a good edge, for example?). Some people are totally against stainless steel, saying that it will never give a good edge. The first thing to bear in mind is that different tasks require different types of edge. You could never cut a 2-inch piece of manila with a straight-edge razor, and if you tried you would ruin the razor forever. I differentiate between the razor sharp edge I put on my pocket knife and use for cutting and trimming small stuff and the saw-like edge which I put on my bench knives for cutting ropes and cables. I get the razor edge by sharpening it on a softish fine stone, and the saw-like edge by sharpening it with a very coarse stone or a steel.

As far as a lubricant for the stone is concerned (and of

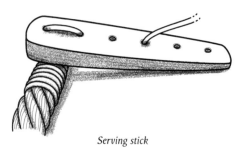

Serving stick

course there must be a lubricant to stop the pores of the stone clogging up) I use water, but this can only be used if you start with a new piece of stone. If the stone has already been used with oil, I use kerosene with a touch of oil. I believe that a knife will only hold its edge for a long time if it is never used, so a frequent tickle on stone or steel, and not allowing the tool to get into too bad a state, is by far the better practice.

As far as the argument between carbon and stainless steel goes, it is worth remembering that there are many variations of both. I have knives in both materials that I find work for me. Often these are just basic utility knives, as used by butchers or fishermen, but it should be borne in mind that at sea, salt water soon ruins the best of carbon steel knives unless great care is taken to keep them dry and clean.

Knots

Some knots are almost tools in themselves.

Constrictor knot

Works well as a temporary seizing, holding together the end of a rope, a bundle of lines before making a button knot, building the core of a fender, and many other examples. When pulled really tight you may have to cut it to remove it. However, when you understand the structure of

the knot it is possible to untie in many circumstances with the help of a fid or spike.

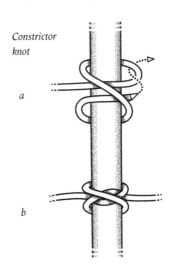

Constrictor knot

a

b

Packer's knot
Based on a figure eight, this knot works well when making up such things as fender bases, because the more you pull, the tighter it grips. It can be locked with a half hitch, to make it secure.

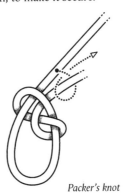

Packer's knot

11

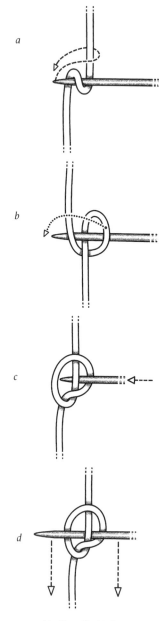

Marlinespike hitch

The best way of pulling fine line extra tight without cutting your fingers. The direction of pull is important; if you make the knot in the wrong direction or pull in the wrong direction the hitch slips.

Bundles

When working with long lengths of line it is helpful to make them up into bundles. There are many ways of doing this, but just wrapping the line round your hand and holding the bundle in place with a rubber band works as well as anything. You should start the wrapping near the work and hank round your hand till you get to the end; with a bit of luck the line can be pulled out from the center of the bundle as you work. If things start to get into a mess, sort them out and rehank before you have a completely knotted mess of a bundle.

Gunk, goos, tar, etc.

Tallow

A touch of tallow on your fid or spike is a great help. It only needs a little. You can make your own tallow by saving the fat from your roast beef or lamb (pork is no good). Put the congealed fat into some water, boil it up, and when it has cooled and gotten hard, skim it from the top. Repeat once more and this should remove most of the impurities. You will also find that tallow will help

Marlinespike hitch

clean your hands of Stockholm tar. A blob rubbed into the hand then wiped off onto a cloth will get rid of most, and then soap and water should do the rest.

Linseed oil

This is good for "feeding" wood and, mixed with Stockholm tar, can be the base for a treatment for rigging. It is worth knowing that there are two types of linseed oil, boiled and raw. The boiled oil will go off and harden almost like paint. "Raw oil soaks right in, boiled oil forms a skin."

Rigging mixtures

I do not think that rigging mixes are particularly scientific. Use a mixture of perhaps 2 to 1 of Stockholm tar to boiled linseed oil, with a touch of dryers if possible to help it go off. If the tar is very thick and you want it to penetrate into fibers or right into the core of the wire you may wish to add some real turpentine to the mixture. There is no need to add the whiskey given in the recipe in Brady's Kedge Anchor 1849:

> For blacking ship's standing rigging: To half a barrel of tar add 6 gallons of whiskey, 4 pounds of litharge, 4 pounds of lamp black, 2 buckets of boiling beef pickle, or hot salt water out of the coppers, if the other cannot be had conveniently. Mix well together and apply immediately.

The purpose of any rigging mix is to protect the rope and wire from moisture. Some people paint seizings and servings in a contrasting color as a decorative feature.

Stockholm tar

This can still be obtained from tack shops and veterinary sources, where it is still used on the hooves of animals.

Paints and varnishes for decorative work

In the old days, when only natural materials were used, everything had to be protected from the weather. The quality of the materials may not always have been the best, so paint was used both to protect and highlight decorative knots, and whole bell ropes would be painted. Ropework on tillers would have been varnished.

If you use natural materials today it is worth remembering this, and you may wish to treat your ropework in the same way. If you have the time and inclination you can do the same on any synthetic lines used. Take care, as varnishes change the color of materials quite dramatically. Many yacht varnishes will make a flax or hemp line go very dark brown, like a tarred line, and will turn a white line a golden color. I have found that some of the varnishes based on either acrylic or PVA (which allow the brushes to be cleaned in water and are sometimes sold as "low odor") only slightly darken the work. Do some tests first to avoid ruining your work.

Melted ends of synthetic rope

Do not make great blobs of melted plastic on the ends of your lines; they will crack and, when running through your hands, can do great damage. If the ends are to be melted, do so in a minimal manner, taking care to smooth the end with wetted fingers. Polypropylene has a fairly low melt point and is not too much of a problem if a quick heat is applied, but nylon and polyester have much higher melt points and can burn your fingers very easily. BE CAREFUL.

Measuring rope

In the past, rope was measured by its circumference rather than its diameter, and you can see why when trying to measure a large rope. In the UK and Europe today rope is measured by its diameter in millimetres. As a rough guide you can convert from one to the other by saying that the circumference in eighths of inches is equal to the diameter in millimetres. It is well worth noting that today in America rope is sold by its diameter in inches, but for over 2 inches in diameter measurements change over to circumference. Wire rope has always been sold by its diameter, even in the UK.

Cordage

The right kind of rope for the right job will make all the difference both to the making and the finished product. I do not come from the school that says that natural fibers are best. I think that you should use the appropriate rope for the job. It's worth the trouble searching for the best materials and usually worth paying extra for quality, be it in natural or synthetic material. Good natural materials have a certain feel that is rewarding and can give the item you've made the appearance of coming from the past. But natural materials will rot quite easily and a fine job can soon look very shabby, thus wasting a great deal of work. It is worth exploring the various imitation natural materials for jobs that are subject to rot, but even they are not going to last forever. I like to use a material that is fairly firm and gives good definition to any knots that are tied in it. If you are splicing, it is helpful that the strand itself holds its twist, but you do not need the lay to be so hard as to start to wrinkle and distort as you splice.

I give some idea as to the sort of material to be used in each of the projects, but you may have to adapt to those materials that you can find. This is nothing new; sailors doing fancy knot work 150 years ago would have had to make do with whatever they could lay their hands on.

The source for fine materials can be difficult to find, and you may need to use a number of places to get a variety of materials. Look in Yellow Pages under ropes and twines. Some of the companies will only supply in bulk, but it may be worth visiting them if they have the sort of materials you are looking for. Actual rope manufacturers normally only supply in bulk with high minimum orders, but if you have some big projects it may be worth talking to them; they can always send you to one of their suppliers. Farming supply shops or yacht chandlers can also be a good source as, although they may not have natural mate-rials, they may be able to put you on to a good source. Fisherman's stores and cooperatives may also have a good range of interesting materials. Sailmakers and riggers may well sell you short lengths of rope and the odd ball of small stuff. Then there are also a few specialist mail order suppliers (see appendices). Keep your eyes open when travelling and buy when you see the kind of materials that you like, lay-ing down, like fine wine, the best of twines and cord for that special project. Just keep your cordage dry, dust free, and away from insects or other pests and you will bless the day that you bought those special items.

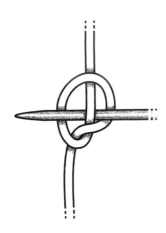

Simple Key Ring

This combination of the single and then the doubled boatswain's whistle lanyard knot has a simple beauty. I must have made tens of thousands over the years and I am still satisfied each time I make one. As well as being used as a key ring decoration or identifier, it works very well as a shackle release, or a zip pull, although you may then prefer to make it in heavy thread. With the addition of the appropriate fitting, a pair will make pretty earrings; green and red will give you port and starboard. Use ⅛" for the big earring look, heavy thread for a fine look, and if you really want to struggle, work with even smaller line. At the other end of the scale, tied in something like ¼" line, you will have a basic bell rope. You could also make a couple of the single knots before the double to make it longer.

I like the name "boatswain's whistle lanyard knot," but this self-same knot can be known by a number of other names: the two-strand diamond knot or sailor's lanyard knot. Whatever name you use, this knot is closely related to the Chinese button knot, said to be the most tied knot in the world; you might believe it when you think of all those Chinese jackets with their knotted buttons.

Materials

1 yard of ⅛" line of your choice
1" or 1¼" diameter split ring or key ring

Knots used

Boatswain's whistle lanyard knot: diagrams a and b
Double boatswain's whistle lanyard knot: diagrams a and c

Method

Fold the line in half, and holding the bight make the single version of the boatswain's whistle lanyard knot (**a** and **b**). Tighten so as to leave just a small loop for the split ring, then make a second knot, but this time double it (**a** and **c**). Work it up tight, leaving a small space between the single and double knots. Trim the ends with a knife and fit the split ring.

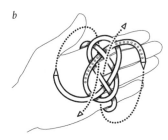

b

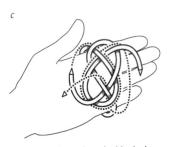

Boatswain's whistle lanyard knot

c

This shows the path to double the knot, both ends need to follow round

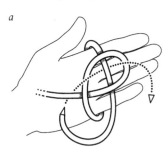

a

Start of boatswain's whistle lanyard knot

If you are using this as a zip pull, use either a smaller split ring (really small stainless steel split rings can be purchased from a fishing supply store), or start by threading the line through the hole in the zip tag.

Shackle Release Lanyard in Portuguese Sennit

I was asked to copy this simple but practical lanyard for use as a pull release on certain types of shackles. Notice that after the two sets of movements the two ends form a reef or square knot. Another name for this sennit is square knotting, and yet another is Solomon's Bar. It is the basis of all macramé or, as some sailors used to say, 'McNamara's lace'. Look out for the belt on page 81.

If just one step is repeated, without the second reverse step, a twist develops in this sennit. That's fine if it's what you want, but *you* should be the one who decides.

Tied in ⅛″ line and fitted to a split ring, this will also make a fine simple key fob, or zip pull.

If you start with one strand tied round the bight of a second, giving 4 ends after you have made your Portuguese sennit, the ends could be finished with a lanyard knot (page 84) that will act as a button to make a bracelet.

Materials

1 yard of ⅛" braided synthetic line

Knots used

Portuguese sennit flat: diagrams a and b
Portuguese sennit spiral: diagrams a and c

Method

Middle the line and hold together about 4" from the bight. You can do this with your fingers or use a fine piece of twine to make a temporary seizing.

a

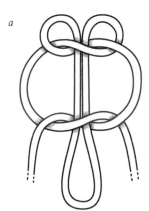

b

Flat Portuguese sennit

c

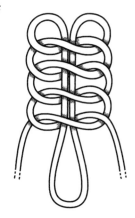

Start the Portuguese sennit (decide whether you want it flat or spiral) and continue until you have about a 1½" loop left. The ends can either be trimmed off close and melted to stop them coming undone (mind your fingers) or pulled back inside the sennit alongside the core using a loop of wire or fine line.

Spiral Portuguese sennit

19

Deluxe Key Ring

Really a miniature bellrope, this was first put together by my wife Liz. Tied in ⅛" as shown it is very handsome, the star knot being one of the world's almost perfect decorative knots which is not too difficult to tie if you take it one stage at a time. I find it a little bit awkward to make in heavy thread or smaller, but it still looks great.

By making the body longer and perhaps using heavier line you'll have a simple bellrope that will draw admiring remarks from all.

Materials

3 x 1 yard of ⅛" line
1 x 1" or 1¼" split ring

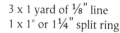

Knots used

3 strand plait (just like a hair braid)
A temporary seizing, probably a constrictor knot: page 11
3-strand diamond knot or crown and wall knots tied in pairs: diagrams a and b
Alternate crown sennit 3 and 3: diagram c
6-strand star knot: page 23
Doubled crown finish: page 24

Method

Seize the 3 lengths of line together just off-center and make a short length of 3-strand plait. Fold over and temporarily seize together to make a loop. Undo any spare plait, arrange the 6 ends into 3 sets of 2, and make the diamond knot (crown and wall) with these pairs. Work tight up to the loop and remove the temporary seizing.

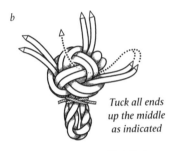

b

Tuck all ends up the middle as indicated

through the center. This little button on the end is called a doubled crown (see page 24) Finish by trimming the ends close to the base of the star knot.

(If you want to use ⅛" to make a 6" bellrope you will need 3 x 6½ feet.)

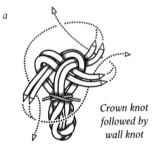

a

Crown knot followed by wall knot

With every alternate strand make a crown knot, then crown with the remaining 3 strands. Keep this up until you have about a 1½" length of 3+3 crown sennit, then tie the 6-strand star knot (page 23). Work tight and finish with a 6-strand crown knot, pulling the ends down

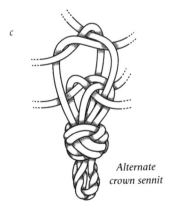

c

Alternate crown sennit

Bellrope Worked with 6 Ends

This is the first commercial bellrope I created, and I am still making it today. I needed money to get married, so to augment my income by making a few bellropes, I made up a couple of samples in some heavy nylon thread and took them to the prestigious yacht chandlers in the West End of London, Captain O. M. Watts. Their buyer looked at my samples, said that they were far too thin, but went on to describe the sort of thing he might be interested in. I went away and made up this design using ⅛" cord. That first one took about 1½ hours to make.

This time the buyer liked it, and said he would give me an order. As he wrote down 3 in his order book I thought, "Is that all, after all this work!" Then he wrote "dozen"! So, my first order was for 36 bellropes each taking about 1½ hours; my first introduction to mass production. Practice certainly speeds up the making of any item!

The first main knot, the Matthew Walker knot, is one of my favorites, although it takes quite a bit of time to tie and form into shape. You could, of course, replace it with a quicker knot such as the diamond in pairs that I used at the start of the deluxe key ring (page 20).

Materials

3 x 6½ feet of ⅛" line

Knots used

3 strand plait (just like a hair braid)
A temporary seizing, probably a constrictor knot: page 11
A Matthew Walker knot in 6 strands: like page 74
Alternate crown sennit 3 and 3: page 21
Diamond knot/crown and wall in 6 strands: like page 21, 77
3-strand crown knot: like page 50
Crown sennit with 3 pairs: like page 26
Star knot with 6 strands: diagrams a, b and c
Double crown finish: diagram d

Method

Start as you would for the deluxe key ring. Seize the 3 lengths of line together just off-center and make a short length of 3-strand plait. Fold over and temporarily seize together to make a loop. Undo any spare plait, arrange the 6 ends spread out neatly and separately, and starting with a

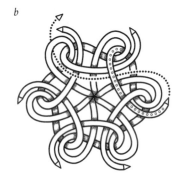

b

All strands need to be tucked as shown

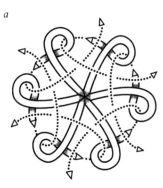

a

Star knot start

6-strand wall knot, go on to make a 6-strand Matthew Walker (page 74).

Work tight up to the loop and remove the temporary seizing. Now make 1⅞" of 3+3 crown sennit (page 21). Tie with 6 strands a diamond knot (crown first then wall below), double this knot, and work it tight and even.

c

Tuck all ends up the middle as indicated

With every alternate strand make a 3-strand crown knot, tighten so that it beds down into the center of the diamond knot, then go on to make a series of crown knots with 3 pairs of line, crowning always in the same direction, until you have about 3" of crown sennit in pairs. Tie the 6 strand star knot, work it tight and finish with a doubled crown (diagram d), trimming the ends close to the base of the star knot. If you prefer to finish with a tassel stop at the star knot, just fray out the ends and trim to length; dunk in very warm water, to help get rid of the kinks in the yarns.

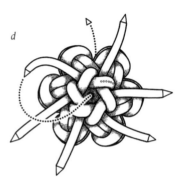

d

A crown knot doubled by pulling all ends down the middle as shown

Bellrope Worked with 8 Ends

I call this our 11-inch bellrope, but you can make it longer or shorter, add Turk's heads, and interweave color to change its style. Once you've got the hang of the 8-strand square sennit it grows quite fast, so combined with the crown sennits it makes a long bellrope fairly quickly. The first time it may take you 2-3 hours to complete . . . with a bit of luck!

I usually stop after the 8 strands crowned in pairs, but you could add another section with the 8 strands crowned singly; this will leave a space in the core of the sennit, so you will need to put in some sort of filler, perhaps a bit of ⅛" line if you are using ⅛" for your sennit. Sometimes I make up the end globe knot and follow it round a second time, then introduce a second colored strand for the other two passes; this shows off the complexity of the globe. With a 3-lead 5-bight or 4-lead 5-bight Turk's head above in the same colored line, it really makes a deluxe bellrope. Use your imagination to try out all sorts of combinations of the knots and sennits I've used here.

Materials

4 x 10 feet of ⅛" line for the basic bellrope
1 x wooden ball about 1½" in diameter
Extra lengths of ⅛" of a differing color for Turk's heads or interweaving of the globe knot end

Knots used

4 strand round sennit: page 49
Diamond knot with 4 pairs: like page 21
8-strand square sennit: diagrams a and b
Diamond knot/crown and wall with 8 strands: like page 21, 77
Alternate crown sennit 4 and 4: like page 21
Star knot with 8 strands: like page 23
Crown sennit with 4 pairs: diagram c
8-strand globe knot ball covering: diagrams d and e
Optional Turk's heads decoration if required 3-lead 5-bight: page 30

Method

Start as the deluxe keyring (page 20) but this time make the loop (page 49) using 4-strand round sennit and the diamond knot with 4 pairs of line (page 21). Then make about 2¼" of 8-strand square sennit, apply a temporary seizing and make an 8-strand diamond knot doubled (page 21, 77). Then follows 2¼" of alternate 4+4 crown sennit (similar to the 3+3 on page 21 but a little harder to get to sit well), an 8 strand star knot (similar to the 6 strand on page 23), then 2½" of 4 strand crown sennit with pairs. Finally, starting from an 8-strand wall knot, tie the handsome 8 strand

a

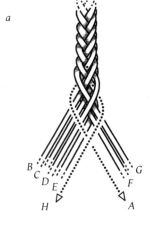

Start with 3 strands on one side and 5 strands on the other. First take A across front then take H across front

b

....Do the same behind, take B across, then G across

globe knot for the end, following the knot around again before putting in the wooden ball. Complete the piece by following around this knot twice more (a total of 4 times). This globe knot

d

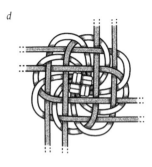

The fancy 8 strand crown shown on top of the 8 strand wall knot

takes a minimum of 22" of line, so make sure that the shortest of your 8 strands is at least this long before you start. If you wish, add extra colored Turk's heads at any place on the bellrope.

c

Crown sennit in pairs

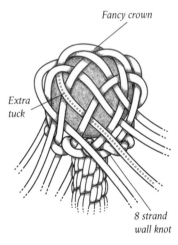

Extra tucks after the fancy 8 strand crown on top of 8 strand wall makes the globe knot

A Simple Side Fender

"Any piece of cable that is cut off, most commonly any part of an old cable, is called a junk. Such as this they hang for fenders by the ships sides."

So wrote Sir Henry Mainwaring in 1623 in his *Seaman's Dictionary*, the earliest Nautical Dictionary in English. Today it is still a good way to make a beefy side fender for a barge or tug, I have made them using old ships mooring cables, and offcuts of heavy coir from wrap-round fenders. The cable may be just stitched together with some line, but I prefer to either make a proper seizing or even better, if I have the time, to make two or three Turk's heads round the cables thereby giving these simplest of fenders that proper seaman's look. I think that 3 or 4 hanging over the side can really look quite smart and not cost a great deal.

If you use your imagination, the same idea can be developed to make a fender with lanyard at each end, so it can be hung lengthways to protect the leeboard on a barge.

Materials

For this type of fender you can use whatever rope is at hand, but here are the requirements for a couple of basic variations:

A   2 x 6½ feet of 2½" square plait old ships' mooring cable
    3 x 26½ feet of ½" polypropelene for the seizings
    1 x 10 feet of ½" polypropelene for the lanyard
B   1 x 6½ feet of 3⅞" (actual diameter) coir
    3 x 25 feet ½" manila for the Turk's head
    1 x 10 feet ½" manila for the lanyard

Knots Used

Constrictor knot; page 11
Flat seizing: diagrams a, b, and c
Or 3-lead 5-bight Turk's head: diagrams d, e, and f

Method

Fold both pieces of the heavy cable in half, making the bend as tight as possible by giving it a good beating with a heavy mallet. If you are using very heavy coir you will find that it is much harder than ships cable to bend; you may well have to resort to a Spanish windlass or, ideally, that rarest of beasts, the rigger's screw. If you are using 2 pieces of cable, put the 2 pieces together with the bends at the same end. Hold the folded rope or ropes in place with a couple turns of a

a   b   c

Flat seizing

temporary binding of some sort; my favorite is a constrictor knot, as you can pull the ends and the whole thing cranks up nice and tight. Now put on the permanent seizing of 7 or 8 turns. I start with a constrictor knot around either all strands or, for very heavy rope, a constrictor around one strand. Pull very tight on each turn; finish off with a couple of frapping turns and lock in place as in the diagram. Alternatively, 3-lead 5-bight Turk's heads followed round 3 times will serve a similar purpose and look even more handsome. It will help to first practice tying the Turk's head round your fingers. You can use your thumb to hold the turns in place. You are making a 3-strand continuous plait or sennit. When all the seizings or Turk's heads are in place trim the bottom; you

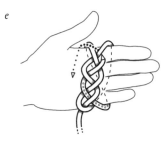

e

will need to sharpen your knife a few times to get through this heavy rope. I use a very coarse stone with water as a lubricant to sharpen my favorite knife. For the very heaviest of ship's cable I sometimes even resort to a hacksaw to get through the rope. After the end has been trimmed, all that remains is for the lanyard to be fitted with a splice through the top loop, then you can whip or back splice the inboard end of the lanyard and hang over the side to protect your craft.

d

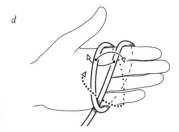

f

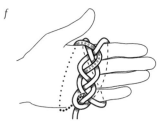

3-lead 5-bight Turk's head

Side Fender
Using the Crown Sennit

There are many ways of making a side fender, all using the crown sennit, put together in various ways. This is the way I usually do it.

On board ship, worn out old rope would have been used, whereas shore-based fendermakers would have used new material, certainly on the outside. Coir has always been one of the preferred materials for salt water craft, as it is light (it floats), is fairly resistant to rot in salt water, and for its size is not expensive. If you are making the fender for yourself you can use any old rope that you can get your hands on. Leonard Popple in his book *Advanced Ropework* recommends making a miniature before commencing a full size fender. This both allows you to see how it all goes together and saves the waste of rope. You could always make a giant keyring out of your miniature.

Sometimes people get a little confused between the crown knot and the wall knot (page 33). One is the upside-down version of the other, so it rather depends on how you look at it when you are making the knots. I start work with the top of the fender between my knees and work upwards, so this is the view from which I name the knots. The Swedish fid with its hollow allows the final splicing back to be done both neatly and speedily (I find that a little dab of tallow on the spike dramatically eases the amount of push required).

I have given the amounts of materials needed for a range of sizes. Much bigger fenders can be made by starting with 2 lengths of rope giving 12 strands. A bigger core will of course be needed, and the end crown can be made with pairs of strands.

Materials

All fenders need 3-4m of tarred marline or similar to make the seizing at the start

8" long x 4" diameter fender: 6½ feet of ⅞" coir (no core)
10" long x 4" diameter fender: 8¼ feet of ⅞" coir (no core)
10" long x 5" diameter fender: 9 feet of 1" coir (plus scrap for core)
14" long x 5" diameter fender: 13 feet of 1" coir (plus scrap for core)

Note that coir rope tends to be bigger than its stated size, so if you are using other materials, they need to be a little bigger than the above, e.g., instead of ⅞" coir use 1" manila or hemp and/or make the core a little bigger.

Knots Used

Flat seizing: page 29
6-strand wall knot: diagram a
6-strand crown knot: diagram b
Special 6-strand crown: diagram c
Splicing: diagram d

Method

For an 8" x 4" fender

It is a good idea to make a fender without a core to start with; it gives you one less thing to worry about. Fold the rope in half and put a flat seizing round the bight,

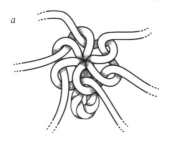

a

6 strand wall knot

to make the eye at the top of the fender. Put either tape or a temporary whipping on each of the 6 rope strand ends and unlay the rope, giving 6 strands to work with. Make a 6-strand wall knot with these ends (diagram a) as this gives the fender a sort of shoulder, then make a series of crown knots on top of each other; (diagram b) this series of crown knots is called a crown sennit, or sometimes just crown-ing. When you have made 6 rows of crown knots , tie the complex 6 stranded crown shown (diagram c). Turn the fender

b

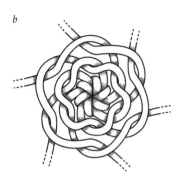

6 strand crown sennit

around and splice the strands back up the outside of the fender to the shoulder. (I find it best to make one complete row of tucks at a time.) When the shoulder has been reached, tuck the ends under the wall knot and out right next to the seizing (diagram d). Trim the ends and roll under the foot to give the fender a good round shape.

c

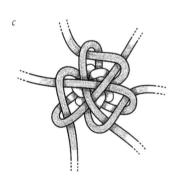

The fancy 6-strand crown

For bigger sizes use a core made up from either 6 or 7 rope strands from the same size rope that you are using for the fender. Once you get going you can use the offcuts from previous fenders. The core is pushed into the hole in the center of the first crown knot and held in place by the subsequent rows of crowning. Trim before making the complex crown at the end. Splice on a lanyard and hang over the side of your vessel.

- Make 8 rows of crowns for the 10" x 4" fender
- 6 rows of crowns for the 10" x 5" fender
- 10 rows of crowns for the 14" x 5" fender

d

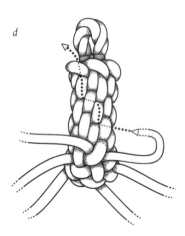

All strands need to be spliced back as shown

Hitching Over a Plastic Fender

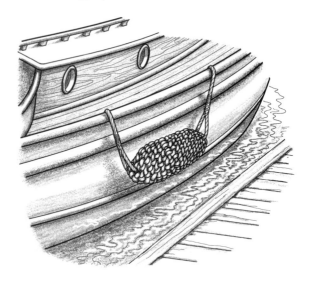

Most rope fenders consist of a core of some kind and a needle-hitched cover. Needle hitching or half hitching as it is sometimes called, is a very versatile covering technique. It can be done using almost any size of material from heavy thread up to 1" diameter line. It is found all over the world covering all sorts of things from tassel heads to clay pots, fenders and knife handles. It has one disadvantage in that it is rather time consuming. So when you start using this technique do not be disappointed at your rate of progress; it does need time and patience. It can take about an hour to use up about 33 feet of ⅜" or ½" line. Be warned, it can be rather addictive; there is a tendency to "just do a bit more."

Covering a small sausage-shaped plastic fender is a good way to learn the technique, and it's a good way to finish up with a traditional looking fender without the extra time and trouble of making up the core. You could of course make up a bundle of old rope with a loop at one or both ends and cover that in exactly the same way. Building up on a plastic fender base is a good idea for larger fenders, as the core will be nearly all air and the finished fender a lot lighter than if a bundle of old rope had been used.

Materials

The hitching of the cover depends so much on the size of the rope and the size of the fender, and on how tight and close the hitches are, that it is only possible to give a very rough guide of the quantity of rope needed. I reckon that about 528 feet of ⅜" or ½" rope will give about a square yard of cover. If you can keep track of the material you use you will get a closer picture for yourself, but you will still have surprises. It always seems to take more material and more time than I estimate!

This means that, to cover a 16" x 5" diameter sausage shape fender, you need about 80-85 feet of ⅜" 3-strand rope.

A 24" x 8" diameter sausage fender needs about 60--66 yards of ⅜" 3-strand rope. This can either be a natural material like sisal, manila or hemp, or a synthetic, but try not to have a too hard-laid (stiff) rope as this makes it more difficult to get the hitches to pull tight and bed down.

It is possible to use braided rope or the strand from a bigger rope but you are then restricted in your method of joining in new ends.

Knots used

Half hitch
Long splice if you prefer to make a spliced join in the rope, but see method

Method

Cut 22 yards of line and tape the ends into 4"-long points. Put the rope around the middle of the fender and adjust to give two equal ends of 33 feet. A 33' length is probably the most efficient length; if shorter there are too many joins and a longer length takes forever to pull through. Start hitching from the center, putting the first row of about 14 hitches for the 5" diameter fender or about 22 hitches for the 8" diameter fender. Space these evenly around one side, then pull the other end tight before locking everything in place by hitching around the second side. Carry on hitching out from the middle, trying to keep the starting point from slipping away from the center of the fender.

When the two sides have used up almost all the rope, assess how much of the fender has been covered and therefore how

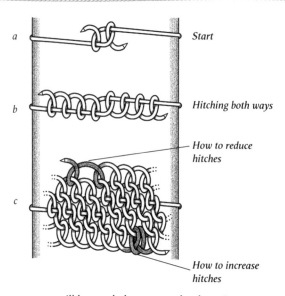

a — Start

b — Hitching both ways

How to reduce hitches

c

How to increase hitches

much more rope will be needed to cover the rest of that side, and make a note of what you think you will need.

This new rope will need to be joined in. This can be done in a couple of ways, either with a long splice, leaving the tails to be trimmed off later, or by bringing the new rope from under a couple of the previous rows and out of the hitch in place of the old short end which can then be covered by subsequent rows. Carry on hitching to the end. As the fender tapers away it's possible to shape the

cover by dropping every second or third hitch, finally burying the end back under a couple of rows of hitching. By seeing how much line was used on the first end you may be able to have a slightly shorter end on the second half, but do not cut too short or you may need to join in yet another short end.

If you want to cover a teardrop shaped fender, it is possible to start at the narrow end and gradually increase the number of hitches by making two hitches in a space instead of the usual single hitch.

Bow Fender

The scale of the bow fender can vary enormously. Whatever the scale, the basic method of construction is the same; there are 2 basic components, the core and the cover. The core takes all the punishment and in many ways it is the fender. The cover is there to protect the core and should look good. Much of the beauty of a bow fender depends on its shape, i.e. the shape of the core, so it is essential that plenty of care be taken when building this up. There should be no lumps or bumps. It can help to finish with a layer of sacking to give a smooth base over which the hitching will go. The 2 side pieces, or "legs," should be symmetrical.

At the heart of the core is a "backbone" rope or chain. For all but the smallest fenders I prefer a chain, but some people use a heavy wire rope and for a light job a backbone of rope will be fine. If you do use rope, use a synthetic material that will not rot before the fender cover has worn out. Fitted to the backbone can be 1, 2, or more short tails that will help to hold the fender up at the bow. It is always disappointing to see a bow fender drooping down; I like to see it tight up and square but occasionally this has to be sacrificed when the fender is needed lower down the stem and there are no appropriate fittings to make the legs fast to.

Half hitching (page 36) is the most versatile method to cover the core. The size of the rope used for this will vary but should be in proportion to the finished fender; ¼" may be fine for a delicate job for a skiff, but ½" for a work boat of 33 to 50-foot length with ¾"-1" for the largest tug fender. The type of rope used depends on taste and material available: 3-strand rope means that you may long-splice lengths together and it can be either natural or synthetic fiber. Natural fiber rope such as manila or sisal, or even hemp, is likely to rot after a few years, especially if the fender is left on all year round. This decay can be slowed down by painting or dunking the fender from time to time in some form of preservative, be it clear Cuprinol, creosote, thinned-down tar, or even old sump oil! It rather depends on how you want the fender to look and how happy you will be to make another one.

Polypropylene is a low-cost synthetic rope that many people use; I quite like the staplespun polypropylene (the slightly hairy-looking one), which is a fair compromise in the cost/look/life stakes. I have seen some handsome fenders in black polypropylene. There are a number of synthetic hemp lookalikes that give a near traditional look, but it is worth checking how resistant they are to UV breakdown, as some are better than others. Nylon or polyester will last the longest but they are often hard laid, which makes hitching hard work; also, they are the most expensive and do have a tendency to look a little modern. A lot of rope is needed and it will take you a lot of time to hitch the cover, but on the other hand I hope you will get pleasure from making the fender.

With all the work of hitching the cover of the fender, you may wish to add a Turk's head at the center to protect the hitching at this vulnerable point. It is easier to replace than having to remake part of the cover, and it certainly gives the fender additional style!

Materials

For the backbone of a fender between 1-2 yards overall: a piece of ¼" or ⅜" short or long link galvanized chain, 1 or 2 shackles, and short pieces of chain (optional) for central suspension points.

For the core: it is sensible to use old scrap rope, in all sizes from ¼" to 2", if you can get hold of it. I prefer to use synthetic rope, as it doesn't hold the water as much, and preferably polypropylene, which is the lightest of the synthetics. It is useful to have all sizes available, and you will use a surprisingly large amount.

For hitching of the cover: lengths of rope based on the guide figures for covering a plastic fender (176 yards of $\frac{3}{8}$"-$\frac{1}{2}$" for 1 square yard).

For a Turk's head rubbing piece: rope of the same or a larger diameter than you used to hitch the cover. A 4-lead 5-bight Turk's head (page 80) followed round 3 times will need approx 18-20 times the circumference of the fender.

Knots used

Constrictor knots: page 11
Packers knots: page 11
Half hitches: page 36
4-lead 5-bight Turk's head: like page 80

Method

Measure the chain to be used, not forgetting that it will be in the center of the fender so it will need to be longer than the inner part of the fender, and allow an extra 6 inches each end for tails outside the fender. Mark the middle of the chain. Rig the chain backbone tight between two swivels at about waist height. If there is a need for suspension chains fit them now with a shackle either at the center, if just one, or a few inches either side of the center if you use 2 suspension chains. A really long fender may have 4 or even 6 suspension chains. Occasionally there is also a call for a chain to hold the fender in place down below the fender.

With the suspension chains rigged, fit 4 thin ropes in the space formed by the interlinking of the chain links. Tie these ropes in place using either a series of constrictor knots or one of the variations of packer's knots. If you have it available, wrap round the 4 ropes and chain with more thin rope, starting at the middle and working out, being sure to treat both sides equally. Unless the fender is to finish up almost straight, remove the wrapped chain from between the swivels and bend it to the approximate curve of the finished fender. Put one long heavy rope to the front of the chain, probably going almost the entire length of the backbone. Put shorter pieces above, below, and behind the backbone to build up the shape of fender you are aiming at. There will always be a little flexibility, but the nearer the correct shape the better. Tie these tightly to the backbone. It is then worth tapering the ends so that there are not

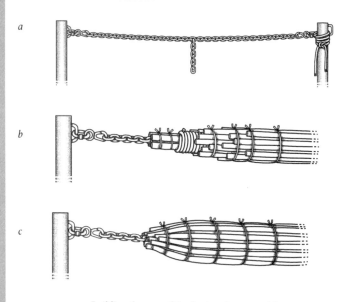

*Building the core of the fender, shown straight,
but could be bent to shape for the later stages if required.*

too many steps where each rope ends. Add extra rope as required to get the shape and size (thinner ropes give a smoother shape); stagger the ends and keep the shape symmetrical. The finished core needs to be about 4 to 6 inches less in circumference than the finished fender size. It is important to get the size and shape right before putting on its jacket.

When you are satisfied with the form and shape of the fender, I find that it helps to cover the whole thing with sacking of some sort, to give a smooth final finish to hitch over. I use hessian, jute, burlap, or sisal sacking if the cover is to be natural and the woven white or cream polypropylene sacking if the cover is to be a synthetic rope. Ideally the color of sacking is somewhere near the color of the rope to be used. This cover is best sewn in place using a packing needle, working out from the middle and getting the cover tight over the core. Some people prefer to wrap the whole fender core with adhesive tape.

You are now ready to cover the core. You can start in the middle and work to the ends, which is fine if the fender is almost straight, but if it is curved I find it best to start at each end and work to the middle. I actually suspend the fender from the leg end, then it is easy to work round and round adding hitches as the fender grows in diameter by putting two hitches side by side into the space of one hitch rather than the usual one. To aid symmetry, work a length of rope on one leg, then change and work on the other. When both sides meet at the center there will be a gap. Hitch round the gap in a circle, dropping hitches as needed until it is completely filled in.

When you have finished hitching the cover (well done!),

you could add a Turk's head in heavier rope round the middle as extra chafe protection. I favor a 4-lead 5-bight Turk's head as I feel it will sit evenly either side of the bow, but a 3-lead version will do almost as well. I have worked to the original 1930s specification for a tug fender that had 5 Turk's heads round it at various points; it certainly looked very handsome when it was finished.

Button Fender
And a few words on narrow boat fenders in general

The narrow boats found on our canals have developed their own special pieces of ropework. Working in and out of so many locks the fenders evolved into a distinct style and shape. On the bow is usually a button fender about 12" diam and about 8" deep, usually with a hitched cover. This fender is used to gently push open the lock gate. On the stern there can be a long fat sausage shape fender, about 24"-28" long and about 10" diam at the center, tapering off each side and called a tip cat. This protects the rudder that sticks out behind the main hull. If one tip cat is not enough, then there can be a second tip cat or another button; there can even be 2 tip cats and a button, a very handsome arrangement when fitted properly with just a little upward tilt. Some boaters prefer to have a single button, which may be a little longer (12 inches) than that used at the bow.

Side fenders tend to be rather on the long thin side (7 inches diam by 12-16 inches long), because in many of the canals there is very little room between the boat and the side of the lock or tunnel wall.

As with all fenders it is very important to make up a good, solid, well-shaped core. The tip cat is constructed very much like the bow fender already described. The button requires a different approach to the building of its core to ensure that it is solid and stable enough to withstand the hard treatment it will receive.

When the button fender is first fitted, it's a good idea to find a quiet spot to very gently push square up against something, to bed the fender in place before it is used in anger!

Materials

For a button fender 12" diameter 8" deep
Scrap rope for the core, preferably synthetic
1 x 4 feet of ¼" chain or 1 piece of 4 feet with a second 4-foot piece
  doubled and joined to the middle of the first chain to give 2 top
  chains
35 yards of ½" rope for the cover (natural or synthetic as you wish)

Knots used

Packers knot: see page 10
Hitching: see page 36
Long splice (if this is your preferred method of joining extra line when
  hitching): like page 56

Method

The core is basically just a solid coil of old rope 9 inches diam by 7 inches high tied nice and tight. The problem is how to make and to tie your coil good and tight. I use a method explained to me by Ike Argent, an old boater who was greatly respected for his well made fenders. A thin metal pipe of about 1" diam is held upright in a vice (a workmate type bench works very well), sticking up through a disc of wood a little over the maximum diameter of the base you want to make. It helps if the disc is marked with a number of concentric circles. Drop 3 or 4 pieces of synthetic cord about ⅛" diam down the middle of the pipe, bring their other ends down the side of the pipe, and lay them out evenly around the base with their ends hanging down the sides of the disc. Start wrapping the core

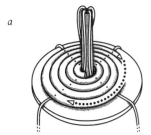

a

Note: the ties go down the center of the pipe

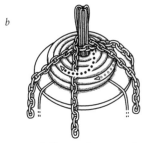

b

Coiling up the core and putting in the chains

material around the pipe keeping the thin lines in place. If your core material is all the same diameter you can build up your coil in a series of flat discs, working out to the required size (9 inches) then back in again. When the disc is about half the height of the fender, place the chain or chains in the middle and carry on up to the top of the button fender base (7"). If you are using a variety of material to build up your core, you can wrap it round the pipe to the height (7") required and work back down again to the base. This way you will have to put the chain in the middle and wrap up and down round it until you reach the 9" diam wanted.

When the core is the right size, pull out the cord ends that are down inside the pipe and tie each end to its own other end with a packers knot, giving a good heave tight as you do. Remove the pipe, bed the rope down with a few blows with a mallet, and apply extra bindings to ensure the core will hold together come what may. You may wish to cover this base with some sacking; it certainly helps to hitch over a smooth surfaced core.

Put the middle of the cover rope around the middle of the fender core and start hitching out each side. When you reach the edge of the core, decrease by skipping every third hitch for a whole row. Then make a full row skipping every fourth hitch, and finally skip every other hitch until you reach the center and finish by burying the end, bringing it right out to the edge. Give the fender another good beating with a mallet before finishing the other side in the same manner.

All that remains is to fit the fender good and tight to the boat. It is a good idea to saw through one of the links of the chain so that, should a fender get caught in a lock, the chain gives way before the boat ends up under the water.

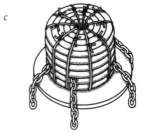

The core all finished and tied up

A Simple Lanyard

A tool dropped when working aloft is bad news--at best a damaged deck, at worst serious injury to a fellow crew member. If it falls over the side it's gone forever and at sea there is no local chandlery to take more of your hard-earned cash for a replacement. The best and safest thing to do is to keep your tools on a lead, then they cannot run away. Fit them with a lanyard!

Here is a simple lanyard with just a little decorative detail, that goes round the neck and allows the knife or other tool to slip into a pocket or sheath. Make the lanyard long enough so that you can stretch your arm out fully, with a loop that will fit easily over your head. It is possible to make the knots sliding so as to adjust the loop, but a sliding knot on this kind of lanyard is not a good idea. In fact it is a better idea to have a weak link between tool and lanyard, as it is no good saving your tool at the expense of strangling yourself. Made a little longer and adjustable, if you wish, the whole lanyard can go right around the waist with a clasp knife on its end that slips neatly into a pocket.

The same style of lanyard, perhaps with a whistle on its end, can go round the shoulder and into the breast pocket of a uniform. By using heavier rope, say $3/8''$ with a clip fixed to the smaller loop and making the other loop just big enough to put your hand through, you will have a dog lead--or is it a dog lanyard?

Materials

For a neck lanyard: 6½ feet of 3/16" 3-strand rope
For a dog lead: 6½ feet of ⅜" 3-strand rope and a clip

Knots used

Eye splice start: diagram a
Diamond knot/crown and wall doubled: diagram b

Method

Put a temporary seizing about 8" from the end of the rope, then unlay the 3 strands, taping the ends so that they do not come undone. Form a loop of about 2¾" and tuck the 3 strands as in the start of an eye splice.
Now make a crown knot around the rope, followed by a wall beneath the crown, thus making

a diamond knot. Double the diamond knot and then treble if you like. Now repeat the same

b

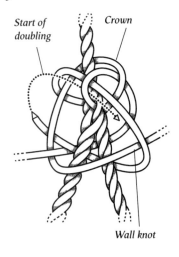

Start of doubling

Crown

Wall knot

knot but this time make a big (about 20") loop at the other end. Check the fit of the lanyard for yourself by holding the little loop in your outstretched hand, to get the perfect length of neck loop before making the splice start.

a

The eye splice start

If you wish you could make an extended diamond knot by putting an extra tuck after making the crown and the wall (see page 50).

By missing out the spliced start and going straight to the crown and wall around the rope, your lanyard will slide, but as I have said before, think first and watch out: It may be OK around your waist or shoulder but not around your neck.

If it is a dog lead/lanyard that you want to make, use 5-6½ feet of ⅜" 3-strand rope and a clip. Don't forget to fit the clip before making the small loop.

A Fancy Lanyard

For something special, be it a handheld compass, compact
camera, bosun's call, or special knife, it is good to have a lanyard that
will speak silently of the skills of its maker. Long before there were
certificates of competence for sailors, a man would have been judged
by those little displays of skill to be seen in his knife lanyard or sea
chest handles. Today many traditional boat festivals operate a system
of passes that are worn on a piece of string around the neck. I first
developed this lanyard to wear my pass at the huge maritime
festival held at Brest in 1992. It is not often that I have time to make
something for myself, being busy making things for others; I made the
"Brest lanyard" on the ferry to France. It has served me well ever since
and has led to variations that can be used for other personal items.
With a short "tail," it suits a coach's whistle or identity pass; with a
longer tail it would suit a hiker's pocket compass. Make the tail longer
still and your knife should not go for a swim.

Materials

For a short-tailed lanyard: 1x 16½ ft and 1 x 33 ft of ⅛" line
For a long tailed lanyard: 1 x 20 ft and 40 ft of ⅛" line

Knots used

Portuguese sennit: page 19
Spiral Portuguese sennit: page 19
Diamond knot: page 21, 77
4-strand round sennit: diagram a and b
Diamond knot spliced: page 46
Extended diamond: diagrams c and d

Method

b

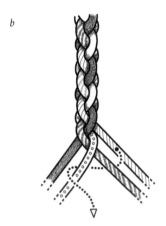

Fold both pieces of line in half, seizing them together to make a pair of loops about 2½" overall and giving you 4 ends (2 long and 2 short). Make a diamond knot (crown first then wall below (see page 21, 73), double by following round, then take hold of the seizing and work the diamond knot tight. When this has been done you will have the loops which will hold the item that you don't want to lose. If you prefer only one loop at the

a

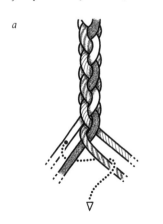

4-strand round sennit

end there are 2 solutions; one is that after tightening the diamond knot you could cut out the spare loop; or the other, a much more seamanlike way, is to work the spare loop right down out of sight into the middle of the diamond knot. Now with the 4 strands make a length of 4-strand round sennit about 3¼"- 4¾" long for a short lanyard or 14" for a longer lanyard.
If you wish you can stop along the length of this bit of sennit and pop in another diamond knot and/or any other fancy

c

Crown knot start for diamond knot

4-strand knot--a star knot or a Matthew Walker, perhaps. The next part will form the neck loop. Start by making about 2¾-3¼" of spiral Portuguese sennit (page 19) then 24" of flat Portuguese sennit (this is the bit that actually sits around the back of your neck). Finally make another short length of spiral Portuguese sennit, this time making the twist the opposite way to the first piece of spiral sennit . You should now have 4 shortish tails which you can

splice into the last bit of the 4 strand round sennit before making a tucked diamond knot of 4 strands (see simple lanyard, page 46) or you can make an extended diamond knot by making one extra tuck, follow round 3 times; trim off the ends, whichever knot you choose, and wear your lanyard with pride.

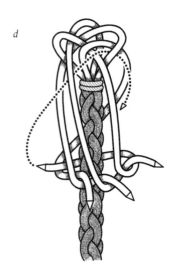

d

Make a wall knot below the crown, then tuck all strands as shown before doubling to make an extended diamond knot

Binocular Strap

Binoculars and many cameras need a strap or lanyard that has loops at both ends and will sit comfortably around the back of the neck. This strap uses the width of the Portuguese sennit to take the weight on the neck and the flexibility of 4-strand round sennit for the rest of the piece. As both sides of the strap must match it has to be worked out from the middle, giving the problem of making little loops on each end. The principle of the solution described here was first pointed out to me by Paulo Escudeiro from Portugal, and it can easily be adapted to make loops on the ends of lanyards and other items that have 4 or more strands. These loops could be made directly onto the fixing rings of the binoculars, or you may wish to fit small split rings that can in turn be fitted to the fixing points. Make the strap as long as you like; camera straps are usually longer than binocular straps, but you are the one making it, so do what suits you.

Materials

2 x 11 feet of ⅛" cord
2 x 6½ feet of ⅛" cord
2 split rings of about ⅝" are required unless you attach directly to the
    camera or binoculars

Knots used

Diamond knots: page 21, 77
Portuguese sennit flat: page 19
Spiral Portuguese sennit: page 19
4-strand round sennit: page 48
Crown loop ends: diagram a

Method

If you start at the middle of the strap you will have to handle shorter pieces of line and so make a quicker, easier, and hopefully neater job. At the middle of the 2 shorter pieces, temporarily tie the center of the longer pieces, and with the long lengths of line commence flat Portuguese sen-

a

*Make a loop before creating the
diamond knot by making a wall knot
underneath and then doubling*

nit one way. Untie your seizing and work the other way using the other long lengths of line. You will need to make at least 6" each way, i.e. 12" in total; you could then do a short length of twisted Portuguese sennit each end, if you wish. Do keep some symmetry to your work. At each end make a diamond knot and double it (page 21, 77). Now make about 10" of 4-strand round sennit each side (page 49) and put on a temporary seizing to stop the sennit coming unlaid while you finish each end of the strap. First do a crown knot and then make an extra tuck to give a loop to go through the fittings on your binoculars or have a split ring put through later. Complete by making a diamond knot and doubling it (page 21, 77). Then fit split rings to the ends so that your strap can be fitted to your binoculars or camera.

Tiller/Boat Hook Covering

To make a good grip on a tiller, boathook handle, mast support post, stanchion, or grab handle is a simple enough job using a series of half hitches. This can be with just a single strand of line, the hitches all going in one direction, which gives a spiral effect and is known as French hitching, French whipping, or grapevine service. If more than one strand is used there are many combinations of either direction of hitch or the number of strands used, giving many patterns. The 2 I show here are named Moku hitching and St. Mary's hitching and were first shown by Brion Toss in *WoodenBoat* magazine about 20 years ago. They are both simple and relatively quick to do and give very distinct patterns. From these basic ideas you can experiment to create lots more patterns. Whatever style or styles of hitching you use, finish each end with a Turk's head.

When all is done you may consider varnishing the work. This is essential if the material you have used to hitch with is natural and is likely to be exposed to the weather, for left untreated it will soon work loose. However, be careful as varnishes tend to change the color of the line used. It is well worth experimenting, by dipping a piece of your line into the intended varnish. Many yacht varnishes will make a flax or hemp line go very dark brown, and will turn a white line a golden color. I have found that some of the varnishes based on either acrylic or PVA, which allow the brushes to be cleaned in water and are sometimes sold as "low odour," only slightly darken the work. In the past this sort of work would have been painted, probably white, with perhaps the Turk's heads picked out in a selection of colors.

Materials

I usually use heavy thread or even smaller on most handles, with perhaps ⅛" material for mast support posts. Irrespective of which method you decide to use, the amount of material required must be determined for each job by taking a yard and making a series of half hitches round the item to be covered. When the yard has all been used up, measure and see how long the piece of hitching is, divide that length into the overall length to be covered, and add say 10% for luck. You now know how many yards you require.
I usually use thicker material for the Turk's heads at each end. Varnish or paint if required.

Knots used

Constrictor knot : page 11
French hitching: diagram a
Moku hitching: diagram b
St. Mary's hitching: diagram c
Turk's heads of choice: pages 30, 62, 63, 64, 80

Method

First work out the amount of material you need (see above) either as one piece for French hitching or divided into 2 ends for Moku hitching, or ⅔ and ⅓ if you are using St. Mary's hitching. You should then make up the line into a bundle or bundles, perhaps held with a rubber band.

Always start with a constrictor knot tied in the material, at the end for French hitching, in the middle if you are going to use Moku hitching, or in the middle of the longer piece and holding the short length

French hitching; always hitch in the same direction

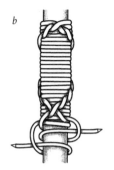

Moku hitching; hitch alternate strands in opposite directions.

St. Mary's hitching; always hitch the strand at the top, all hitches in the same direction.

in place for St Mary's hitching. Then you can start making your half hitches.

As always, keeping an even tension is the key to good looking work. Fine line has a tendency to cut into your hands as you tighten each hitch, so if you intend to cover a long length it would be a good idea to wear gloves or finger protection of some sort. I find a short piece of bicycle inner tube works well if the line I am using is anything but white; other people take preventative measures by wrapping some tape around the fingers that take most of the punishment.

When you have finished hitching, use one of the strands

to make another constrictor knot to hold the end/s secure. Finish each end with a Turk's head covering the constrictor knot.

Things can be a little more complicated if you like the idea of making a selection of hitching styles on a single piece. If in doubt, allow a little extra line to start with. Also, I find it's easier and neater to change from a method using 2 or 3 strands to one that uses fewer strands rather than adding extra strands. You may still need to cover the transition point with a Turk's head.

Varnish or paint the finished job if appropriate.

Grommets for Quoits, Blocks & Sea Chest Beckets

An endless circle of rope called a grommet can be made from a single strand of 3-strand rope just over 3 times the length of the finished ring. This ring or grommet is the essential ingredient for a game of deck quoits [like the game of horseshoes, but using rope rings] or a strap for a wooden block. A pair will make simple sea chest handles or beckets which when decorated with worming, leather, and Turk's heads, add a great deal of style, telling the world that this chest belongs to a real "marlinespike sailor." However they are used, the skill is to get the size correct and then to make the join in such a way as barely to increase the diameter of the rope. This join is the same as that used in a long splice. There are many variations of making it, with each one having its proponents, advantages, and disadvantages, each in their way correct, hence the saying "different ships, different long splices."

Whatever the variation of join used, it helps a great deal if the rope used keeps its form when unlaid. Most natural fibers are fine, but cotton can be a little tricky, while among the synthetics, nylon can give problems. All can be used but the difficult ones need special care.

As one piece of 3-strand rope will provide enough strands to make 3 grommets, deck quoits are usually made up as sets of 3. If you have single and double blocks to strap, always cut the rope long enough to make the biggest strap. When making a pair of beckets, make 3 and use the best pair.

Materials

For a set of 3 quoits:
10 feet of ¾" or 1" diam 3-strand rope, natural if possible

For a pair of chest beckets:
10 feet of ⅝" diam 3-strand hemp, or manila if possible
26½ feet fine tarred marline to worm the rope
The same or larger to make the Turk's heads
2 pieces of approx 3" x 6" leather

For block straps:
1 piece of 3-strand rope 3 times the circumference of the strap plus about 12"

Knots used

For all:
Grommet: diagram a
Long splice join: diagrams b and c

For Chest beckets:
Worming
Turk's heads of choice: pages 30, 62, 63, 64, 80

Method

Having worked out how much rope is required, form a circle in the middle of the rope with the ends overlapping. Mark both parts of the rope at this cross-over point. Now gently unlay one strand from the rope, taking great care to keep as much of the twist, kink, and lay in the strand as possible. It helps to hold the rope up and let the strand that is being unlaid hang down. When you have the strand free, form a circle with the marks of the cross over side by side. Now gently lay one end of the strand round

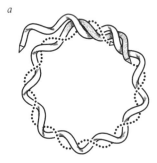

a

Forming a grommet

itself, starting to re-form the structure of the original rope. As the strand is laid into the kink of the lay it may help to give a

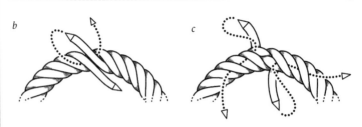

The long splice finish

slight twist to the strand to put back any lost lay. When most of one end of the strand has been used up, use the other end of the strand to complete the 3-strand structure, again gently adding a bit of a twist and perhaps a bit of a push to get the strand to sit neatly. When a complete circle of rope has been made, the 2 ends will overlap. These ends are now joined to give the least increase in diameter possible. Tuck the end as shown, taking a bit of the twist out of the strand as you do. If you tuck correctly the strands should bed down neatly; if you have tucked the wrong way it will stand proud no matter how hard you pull and push. Now tuck each end under one against the lay; leave out half of the strand end and repeat. When all ends are neatly tucked the grommet can be stretched around a large fid (if you have one big enough) or just stretched into a good shape, before trimming the ends. Do not trim too tight because any strain could cause the ends to pop untucked. A more sophisticated join starts with halving each strand end

before making the initial tuck. Make the second and third grommet using the other two strands. Another way to get similar sized grommets that works very well for quoits uses circles of garden wire or similar material measured to a standard length, marked and twisted to join at the mark. Use these rings of wire as a base round which to twist and lay up your rope strand in a manner similar to the above. The wire can be left in the grommets to give a degree of stiffness to the quoits.

Two grommets can be used, as they are, for the most basic of sea chest handles or beckets, or they can be easily decorated by taking a single piece of marline and laying it into the groove of the rope. This is called "worming" the rope. The marline goes around and around, finally meeting the other end, where it can be knotted and the ends tucked out of sight. A piece of leather can be added where the grommet passes under the cleat of the chest. Turk's heads can be added for still more decoration.

A Pair of Fancy Spliced Chest Beckets

The simplest of rope handles for a chest can be made from a piece of rope short-spliced together to form a circle. The short splice gives a greater diameter to the rope and is therefore more comfortable to the hands when lifting a heavy chest. Add a little decoration to this style of handle by making the splice with extra long ends and, rather than trimming them at each end of the splice, these ends are used to make diamond knots round the body of the rope. Chest beckets made like this are quick to do, but still have a bit of style. You can of course go on and add Turk's heads, etc., to your heart's content.

Materials

2 x 5¾ feet of ⅜" or ½" 3-strand rope

Knots used

Short splice: diagrams a and b
Diamond knot: page 46

Method

Decide how large a circle of rope you want to end up with, which will probably be something like 24" in circumference. Before commencing the splice, things can be made easier for tucking by taping or whipping the ends of each individual strand. Unlay both ends of the rope equally and marry these ends by butting the strands together to form a circle of the size you want. Make one tuck with each strand against the lay of the rope in the normal manner. Repeat for the other handle, checking that they are of the same circumference. Tuck each side of the splice 2 or 3 more times. Check that both sets of beckets are the same. With the long tails left, make first a crown knot round the body of the rope and then a wall knot beneath it; double the crown and then the wall, tucking the ends up through the middle of the diamond knot. Work each of the strands tight and trim.

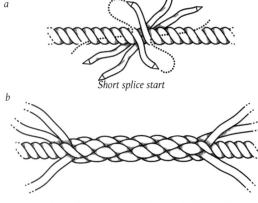

a

Short splice start

b

Short splice with ends ready to make diamond knots

Some Turk's Heads for Decoration or Napkin Rings

Turk's heads are found all over the world in many cultures and are often vested with mystical significance. They come in all sorts of sizes and complexity. They are beautiful knots that provide decoration and a practical purpose when used as grips, splash barriers, and protection against chafe and knocks, or as a purely decorative binding. I find that there are a few that will be useful time and again to cover joins and ends when covering handles with hitching. The odd Turk's head on the handle of a tool gives a sign of ownership, in just the same way that Herman Melville had his pipe made taboo on a Pacific island in the 1840s.

The best way of describing Turk's heads is that they are a continuous plaited ring made with a single strand of line. This single strand version may be followed around as many times as you wish, usually 2, 3, or 4 times. They should not be confused with the manrope knot or diamond knot, both of which are made with the strands of a rope, nor with the monkey's fist which is tripled, quadrupled, etc., as it is made.

To help differentiate among the various Turk's heads, we call the number of loops on its edge "bights" and the number of strands that make up the plait "leads." There are many variations of bights and leads, but early in the 20th century it was independently discovered by C. W. Ashley, G. H. Taber, and L. G. Miller that a true Turk's head cannot be made where the leads and the bights have a common divisor. You can make a 3-lead 4-bight and a 3-lead 5-bight, but not a 3-lead 6-bight Turk's head. J. C. Turner and A. G. Schaake have recently proved the reason for this mathematically in New Zealand.

Whole books have been written about Turk's heads and some people get totally hooked on tying ever more complex variations. There are lots of different ways of setting about tying them. They can be tied round the fingers and slipped over the item to be covered, and they can be tied in much the same way directly around the object.

To make your Turk's heads into napkin rings, tie them in ⅛" hard cord around empty 35mm film cases. To stiffen them, give them a coating of white glue mixed with water 50:50, let them dry, slide off the case, trim the ends inside, and paint inside with more of the PVA glue and water mix.

Here is another Turk's head that you may find useful. The 5-lead 4-bight can be tied around your fingers. Follow the diagrams using your thumb to hold the various passes in place. The earlier passes will lay out a pattern that can be locked into a full over-under design by the last full pass around the fingers.

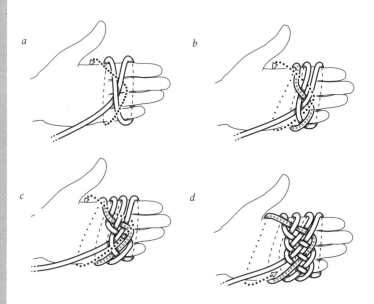

5-lead 4-bight Turk's head

A gadget and some formulae to help make more complex variations

More complex Turk's heads require differing approaches. One is to put pins in a rod as in diagram e, and wrap a fine line round and round from one end to the other, making a dummy pattern and not worrying about the overs and unders. With this basic network complete, use it as a guide to follow and create the overs and unders as required.

It is possible to tie directly round the gadget by following formulae. These can get very complicated, but here are some simple ones that I first saw in Quinton Winch's book *Nets and Knots*.

Make up a rod with 2 sets of 4 pins or pegs in it, as shown in the illustration, one set of pegs to be numbered 1-4, the other to be numbered I, II, III, IV. Starting at peg 1, take your line right around the rod to peg number II, around and back to the left hand side peg number 2, going over and over each time the line crosses the line already in position. Go around back again to the right hand side, going over and over to peg number III. Go from peg III around to peg 3 going under over under over. From peg 3 go around to peg IV going under over under over. From IV go to 4 going over, under, over, over, under. From 4 round to I going over, under,o,o,u,o, and finally complete the full circuit by returning to 1 by going u,o,u,o,u,o,u,o. Having completed the Turk's head, take out the pins before doubling or trebling. This is all shown as follows in diagrams **f**, **g** and **h**.

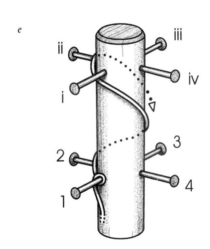

63

Formula for 9-lead 4-bight Turk's head

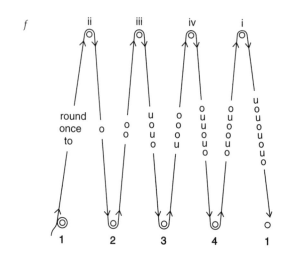

Formula for 13-lead 4-bight

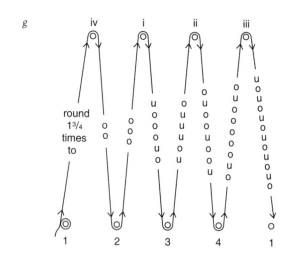

Formula for 17-lead 4-bight

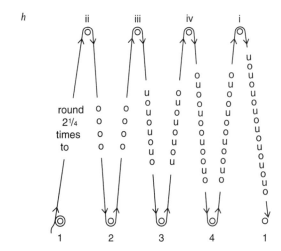

These long complex Turk's heads make an ideal covering for a knife handle; in fact there are many things you can put a Turk's head on. Perhaps you will catch the Turk's head fever just as they did on the Brendan Voyage:

"Every item that could possibly be embellished with a Turk's Head was duly decorated."

Tim Severin, *The Brendan Voyage, 1978.*

Knot Board Notes

It is difficult to trace the actual origin of knot boards, but I think that they were made either as a training aid on board ship or in a Naval training establishment, or as a demonstration of the tyer's skill, either to be displayed in a rigging loft or chandlers or perhaps given away as a gift. Some were made up to be the basis of the illustrations of knot books. Today they are to be found everywhere, many being mass-produced almost on a production line. I have never wanted to mass produce knot boards, preferring to aim at the special "work of art."

There is a certain satisfaction on completing a well balanced layout with examples of one's skills and knowledge, perhaps with a theme or some special appropriate knots for the person you are making it for. Making your own gives you the opportunity to demonstrate your skills and make something individual, a work of art. You can take that extra hour to make a very intricate hitched bottle to act as a center piece. You can make your board have a special theme: knots for climbers, fishermen, true lovers, or maybe just loop knots. I have seen fine boards that show the rigging of tackles, others with a selection of lashings, yet others showing each stage of making a selection of knots and splices.

The first thing to decide is how big you want your board to be. Then what frame you are to use and will it be glazed? Get your frame first, or else you may find that there is nothing deep enough to take that extra special thing you want to put in.

Frames are always difficult and expensive to buy. I have big ones (24" x 36") specially made by a joiner, with a deep moulding and filet strip. I stain and polish them myself. They are a major expense. Small frames can be made up by a picture framer; perhaps you will be lucky to find a sympathetic one who can supply a good deep moulding. The drawings give some ideas as to the variations possible. The filet strip holds the glass in place, and means that it is possible for the board to be shipped and have the glass fitted later.

It also means that in the event of an accident the broken glass can be replaced. For a backing board I usually use $\frac{3}{8}$" plywood covered with felt. I fix the knots with brass pins bought from the model shop. Pins through felt enable you to move and reposition, without a hole showing. I hold the pins with a pair of needle-nosed pliers, and hammer them in with a pin hammer.

I always feel that it is the layout that matters. It helps if there is one special piece of work that acts as a focus. I like to show the knots at work where possible, i.e. bends joining together, hitches to a rod.

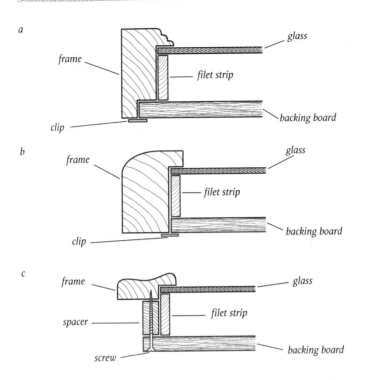

a frame / glass / filet strip / clip / backing board

b frame / glass / filet strip / clip / backing board

c frame / glass / spacer / filet strip / screw / backing board

I only use "bits of brass," etc., to show the working of a knot: a block on a thump mat or a miniature bosun's pipe on a miniature lanyard.

For the knots you can use any material you like. I prefer to use either flax or cotton, varying the size for different knots, usually using ⅛" for the main knots and the same or possibly smaller for the mats, the finest line I can get to hitch a miniature bottle, heavy thread if I do some decorative hitching round a rod. The Turk's heads round that rod can be in heavier thread. Splices need to be made in larger material to be seen, so use ¼" or ⅜" rope. It looks best if all the ends are whipped. I use the finest waxed whipping twine, occasionally using colored twine, perhaps to match the felt background.

Naming the knots is another problem to be solved. Individual brass tags are expensive and it can be cheaper to buy in bulk, but you are then restricted to the same knots. You could use a computer to generate your labels or handwrite them. I stick these labels in place with polystyrene cement. Test your glue on a scrap piece of felt and paper first.

Don't forget to sign and date your finished knot board. One day it will be a piece of history.

Monkey's Fist/Light Pull

Among sailors the monkey's fist is known the world over. It is the knot found on the end of a heaving line. The weight of this handsome knot helps the heaving line to travel farther and more accurately. The monkey's fist has a special significance to the sailor, as his first connection with the land and his helping friend when needing assistance.

It is often confused with the Turk's head but, unlike the Turk's head, it is always spherical in shape and its method of construction is totally different, the full number of passes being defined as it is made. It cannot be enlarged after it has been tied. It helps to have something round in the center to give it shape. This can be a wooden ball or a knot tied in the end of the line and built up with a little yarn to make a ball. In the past it was often a pebble or a bolt or lump of lead, although a dock worker taking a heaving line with what he considered to be a dangerously heavy monkey's fist would cut it off. Today putting a weight in a heaving line is considered to contravene all the safety at work rules.

A good use of the monkey's fist in the home is to make a light pull or blind pull.

Materials

18 feet of ⅛" line will cover a 1½" diam wooden ball with 7 passes
6½ feet of ⅛" line will cover a 1" diam wooden ball with 5 passes
Extra line is needed for hanging

Knots used

Monkey's fist: diagrams a, b and c

Method

If you are using the ⅛" line as a suspension line, add the length of drop you want to the above

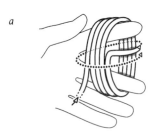

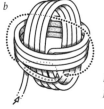

Route of final passes

If you feel that ⅛" line is too heavy as a suspension line, it is possible to drill a ⅛" hole through a wooden ball with a countersunk hole of about 3/16" one end, thread a line of heavy

measurements and start making the monkey's fist round the ball. You will need to make 7 passes or circles on each face of the knot. Use your fingers to make and keep the series of wrappings in some sort of order. Insert the ball after making only two of the final series of passes, then carry on to complete the 7 passes with the ball inside. When the knot has been tied loosely, work all your slack to the longest end, which will be your suspension line. Trim the short end to about ⅜" and tuck it into the body.

Put center 'ball' in before completing final passes

thread through it, and knot the end so it does not pull out but is buried in the countersunk hole. Then cover the ball with a monkey's fist, trimming the ends short and burying them inside.

Monkey's Fist/Doorstop

Tying the monkey's fist in the normal way leaves 2 ends. If a loop is required on the monkey's fist, one end can be formed into an eye and spliced or knotted into a loop, or the ends could be spliced together. To my mind neither of these options is very neat, especially if you wish to make a small monkey's fist key ring.

I first worked out a neat and secure method of making a monkey's fist with a loop when commissioned to make floating monkey's fist key rings, using a table tennis ball as a core. The previous maker had just tucked one end inside, held in place by a dab of glue. It looked neat but, of course, it soon pulled out. To resolve this problem, I introduced a loop by a slight deviation from the usual pattern of turns.

After making hundreds, if not thousands, of these I wanted to make something much bigger that would show off the sculptural form of this special knot. Using ¾" manila, I made the monkey's fist in the same special way, but with a core made up from scrap lead, folded and beaten into shape and then covered with a little spun yarn to prevent the rope becoming soiled as the knot was worked tight. These door stops have proved very popular, and are sculptures in their own right. This exact design can be made into a fender by substituting the ball of lead and spun yarn for a ball of old corks and spun yarn. Whatever the scale of your monkey's fist, be it for earrings, key rings, light pulls, Christmas tree decorations, fenders, or doorstops, you can be certain that if you use this monkey's fist deviation the loop will never pull out.

Materials

For the floating key ring:
1 table tennis ball
13 feet of ¼" rope will cover with 5 passes. I prefer to use polypropylene, either as a hemp look-alike or in the colored multi-filament form, as polypropylene is one of the few ropes that floats

For a door stop:
Scrap lead made up into a ball about 3¼-3½" in diameter, then covered with scrap yarn to bring it up to 4⅜" in diameter
26½ feet of ¾" rope, will cover with 4 passes. I like the look of 3-strand rope for this sculptural project

Knots used

Monkey's fist with a deviation: diagrams a, b, and c

Method

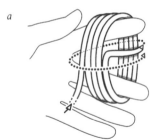

a

Start as standard monkey's fist

It is probably a good idea to start with a key ring version first. This gives you the chance to understand how this monkey's fist deviates from the standard one without having to struggle with the problem of working with heavy ¾" rope as well. The start is as for the standard monkey's fist: first 5 passes around your fingers, then 5 more passes at right angles round the first set, then tuck the work-ing end diagonally through the center, out the other side, form a loop, and tuck the final series of passes from the other side. Put the ball in the middle after just two of these last passes, then complete (diagram c), trapping the ball inside. The whole knot can be worked tight in the usual manner. It is a little tricky follow-ing the hidden diagonal pass out to the loop and back again, but with care it can be done.

When you are happy with your knot, cut the ends off leaving about ⅝" and tuck them into the knot. When you have mastered this, you can

71

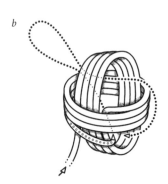

b

*Make the loop before making
the final passes*

tackle ¾" rope to make a door-stop. Heavy rope needs a slightly different approach. You will need to build it up loosely in your hand, using the stiffness of the rope to give some shape to the passes. Put your yarn-covered weight in the middle and complete the final set of passes. I have allowed plenty of material but, even so, you may be slightly short on the first loose tying of the knot. You should gently tighten the knot from the beginning, bringing the slack right through the knot to give you enough rope to complete all 4 of your last passes. Adjust the knot so that all is neat, although a little loose. Now work it properly tight. For this I use

a big Swedish fid to lever out a loop which I take in one hand and with a hammer in the other hand, give a few glancing blows to force through the last of any slack. Working the monkey's fist tight in this way should give you a tight hard knot. When you are satisfied that you have the knot as tight and even as you wish, the two tails can be heaved even tighter using a heaving mallet or heaver (see Tips of the Trade, page 8) before trimming off flush. When all this has been done I hammer the knot into shape making it slightly flat at the bottom. You now have a handsome piece of sculpture that will act as a fine door stop.

c

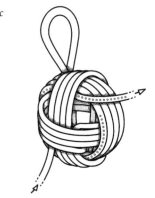

*Put center "ball" in before completing
final passes*

Cat-o'-Nine Tails
(Ditty Bag Lanyard)

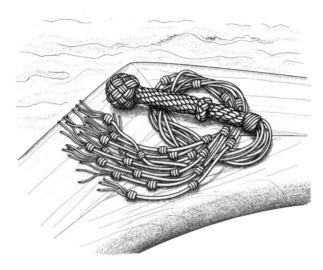

I have yet to see a true cat o'-nine-tails from that brutal period when men could be flogged for the least infringement of discipline. There are a few descriptions but these are hard to decipher. Most cat-o'-nine-tails in museums are someone's interpretation rather than the real thing. The truth is, probably the "cat" was nothing very fancy, but rather just a piece of 3-strand rope with a couple of knots in it to form the handle, then 3 strands opened out into the yarns, and these yarns laid up or plaited into lashes, the tails being knotted at the end to stop their coming undone. It was probably thrown away after use.

The "cat" that I describe here can easily serve as the basis of a ditty bag lanyard; just use 8 tails. This cat-o'-nine-tails is more a decoration than for real use, but mounted on a board it makes a fine trophy, perhaps to be awarded symbolically to the last in a race or to someone who has encouraged improvement in a team. It starts with a Matthew Walker knot, one of my favorites. Here it is tied with 9 lines, which can prove quite a handful, but not impossible using my method, which starts with a wall knot and grows from there. It will work for 3 or more strands. Try it out with 3 or 4 lines to start with and work your skill level up to the 9 slowly.

Materials

9 x 8¼ feet of ⅛" line; I like to use hemp or flax
1 x 1½" wooden ball drilled with a hole of ⅛-¼", or an apparel bead
1 x 5¼" piece of ⅛" stainless steel wire rope, or a nail this long with
  its head cut off, or even a wooden dowel. This is used to stiffen the
  handle. It is possible to just use an extra piece of line but it does not
  work as well

Knots used

Matthew Walker knot: diagrams a, b, and c
Alternate crown sennit, 4 and 4: page 26
Diamond knot/crown and wall with 8 strands: like page 21
8-strand crown sennit: like page 33
8-strand globe knot ball covering: page 27

Method

Cut and measure your 9 pieces of line. Make them into a bundle and put on a temporary seizing about 36" from the end. The first 36" will be your lashes; the rest will go to making the handle. Make a 9-strand Matthew Walker knot with the long ends. I know this will be difficult as you have to handle the long pieces of line but when the knot is tightened it will set better for the rest of the handle. After the Matthew Walker has been tied, continue with the long strands, making an alternate crown sennit with 4 and 4 strands (page 26) round the ninth strand which remains in the middle as a core. Make this alternate crowning for about 2¾", and then with the same strands make a diamond knot (page 21), still keeping the ninth strand as a core.

Take whatever rod you are going to use as a stiffener and work it into the heart of the diamond knot and wrap the ninth strand round it. If the line you are using is a stranded line you can open out the lay a little so it grabs the rod as it is

a

Making the Matthew Walker knot, 3 strand wall knot with first series of tucks

74

b

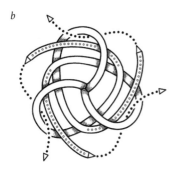

*Second series of tucks completes
a full circle*

c

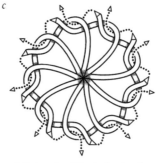

*A 9-strand wall knot, showing the
first series of tucks, 7 more series of
tucks required to complete the 9-strand
Matthew Walker knot*

spiralled up it. With your 8
strands, cover the stiffener
with an 8-strand crown sennit
almost to the end, then push the
wooden ball or bead over the end
of your rod and use an 8-strand
globe knot to cover. You will
need to follow around this knot 3
times to cover the ball completely. Your whip handle is now
complete. You can knot the ends
of the lashes   some sources
say there should be 3 knots per
lash   with simple overhand
knots or blood knots (overhand
knots with an extra couple of
tucks). This would have certainly
made a brutal weapon but looks

fine for decoration. You may
prefer to make a ditty bag lanyard as it is not such a gruesome
project. Make it just like the "cat"
but with 8 strands, the "tails" or
strands being spliced to the
eyelets at the top of the bag,
and a Turk's head slide made
round them to close the neck
of the bag. There is no need for
a stiffener in the handle. As an
alternative to the globe knot you
could finish with a star knot or
a second diamond knot, working
a suspension loop in the manner
of the finish for the binocular
strap (page 52).

A Sailor's Whisk

Sailors would swab the decks daily using giant swabs made from old rope. They would wash the dishes with a miniature version of the deck swab. The table in the fo'c's'le would be kept clean with a whisk made from an odd end of rope. There are a number of ideas as to how these would look in the *Ashley Book of Knots*. This design is based on a whisk brought to me from Nova Scotia. The actual whisk is quickly tied but it takes a while to unlay and comb out the yarns. It should be made from a hard fiber rope such as manila or sisal. I usually use ¾" manila; anything smaller is a bit on the skimpy side. I have made them with 1" rope but the combing time is much longer. Once I made a giant whisk in 2" sisal; it took ages to comb out but looked very handsome.

Materials

34" of ¾" manila or sisal 3-strand rope

Knots used

Constrictor knot: page 11
Wall knot + crown knot to make a diamond knot: diagram a

Method

Fold the rope in half, making a
loop about 4" long by putting on
a constrictor knot as a temporary
seizing. This will be the handle.
Unlay the strands of the rope
and with 2 strands from each
side make a 4-strand crown knot
with the 2 remaining strands
in the middle. Follow with a
wall knot under the crown and
tuck the ends up through the
middle, so making a diamond
knot. Tighten the diamond knot,
taking care not to pull the 2 lazy
strands in the middle, as that
tends to distort the lay of the
rope in the handle loop.

Untie your temporary seizing.
Unlay all 6 strands to the yarns
and then unlay all the yarns
down to the fibers. This takes
time and can make quite a mess,
so best not do it over a clean car-
pet. Use a marlinespike to comb
out any difficult yarns. Now wet
the teased-out fibers and comb
them as straight as possible. As I
make a lot of these whisks I have
made up a kind of coarse comb
with some nails in a piece of
wood. Start by combing out the
ends and working back towards
the knot to comb out all the

fibers. The wet yarns are much
easier to comb than if they had
been left dry. When you are satisfied with the combing out, tie a
constrictor knot round the fibers
about 5" from the diamond knot
and cut off the ends of the fibers.
Slide the constrictor knot off
the end and hang the whisk up
to dry. Finally shake the ends to
loosen any odd stray fibers and
you have a fine little whisk.

a   Crown knot

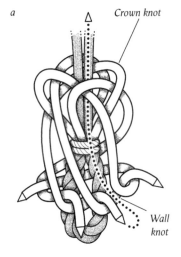

Wall knot

Covering a Wheel

Today's stainless steel steering wheels are all very fine and strong, but they cry out for some sort of rope covering. Not just for appearance, and a well covered wheel can look very handsome indeed, but also for grip and comfort. As one of my customers said, "When it's cold out on the North Sea that's when I feel the benefit of the rope-covered wheel. It's so much friendlier and does not freeze the hands in quite the way an uncovered wheel will." To do this job properly there are a number of things to be done correctly. The first is the choice of material. Much as you may like the idea and feel of natural cordage, it is not really the right thing to use unless you then heavily varnish the wheel, which in some ways defeats the purpose. I always use a synthetic material, which will not change its tension when wet; I use nylon, polyester, or a good quality multifilament polypropylene. Do not use too thick a material; ⅛" diameter is ideal.

The next decision is the actual method of covering the rim. You can use French whipping (page 55), or Moku hitching (page 55). Whichever rim covering method you use, at each spoke you will get a gap. It is here that the 4-lead 5-bight Turk's head made up as a 3-legged covering will make all the difference. This is the detail that gives a proper neat finish, covering that unsightly gap. If when the rudder is square your center point on the wheel is also a king spoke, make a 4-lead 5-bight Turk's head out of perhaps a different color and larger material, so you can find it by feel even in the darkest of nights. Alternatively you can put another Turk's head round the king spoke itself. If the all-square point is midway between spokes then you can add another style of Turk's head at this point. One word of warning: an average wheel takes a lot of line to cover, and fine line cuts the fingers very quickly. You may find it helpful to tape up your fingers before you start, to prevent blisters. Alternatively you can do the job a bit at a time when you have a few days to enjoy doing it.

Materials

⅛" braided nylon, polyester, or a good quality multifilament polypropylene; the quantity will need to be calculated to suit the individual wheel

6½-10 feet of ⅛" material as above to make a Turk's head at the king spoke

Knots used

French whipping: page 55
or Moku hitching: page 55
4-lead 5-bight Turk's head: diagrams a and b

Method

Having chosen the material you wish to use, make a knot at a point 6½ feet from the end and then make a series of half hitches round the wheel until the 6½ feet are used up. Measure the length of the rim that has been covered and calculate from this the amount of material you will need to cover the entire rim of the wheel, adding a little bit extra to be absolutely certain of having enough. Measure off the material to be used and make it up into 1 bundle if you are French whipping or 2 equal bundles joined in the middle if you are going to use Moku hitching. Start by tying a constrictor knot round the rim at a spoke, the king spoke if you know which that is, having one half of the constrictor knot each side of the spoke. You can now carry on making your hitches with either the 1 or the 2 ends, depending on your covering method. Pull each half hitch tight. You will soon realize why I suggested that you put some tape round your fingers, or maybe you will

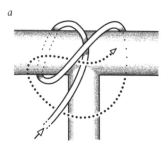

a

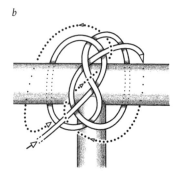

b

4-lead 5-bight Turk's head start

4-lead 5-bight Turk's head ready to be doubled or trebled

be able to take a rest. It is best to stop at a spoke so that the tension is exactly the same for the whole section.

When the complete rim has been covered, tuck the end or ends under the constrictor knot that you started with. Now neaten up each spoke junction point with a 4-lead 5-bight Turk's head, probably followed round 3 times. Dummy up with a dozen slack turns round the rim and add a bit to get the rough amount needed for this knot. Measure the length of material used to make the first Turk's head before you start, so that you can be closer in your measurement for the rest of the knots. Finish off with a Turk's head in $\frac{1}{8}$" line at the king spoke or center position on the wheel. The result will be a very good looking wheel which is much more pleasant to hold than the cold stainless steel.

4-Lead 3-bight Turk's head: This Turk's head is based on the

constrictor knot (see page 11). It is best to practice by tying it round your fingers. By splitting open the knot and making a pass round your hand and tucking under over under, you will finish up with 4 strands plaited together with 3 bights on the edge.

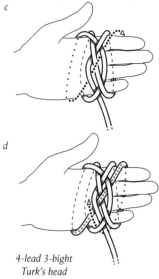

c

d

4-lead 3-bight Turk's head

Belts

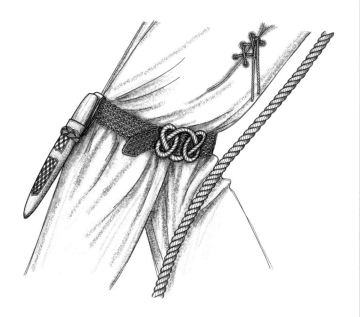

A belt can be as simple as a piece of rope or rope yarn tied around the waist to hold up your trousers or keep your oilskin jacket closed. The late Charlie Brinkley, fisherman and ferryman from Felixstowe Ferry on the Suffolk coast, called such a belt a "Board of Trade belt," a reflection on the probable source of the material. A casual arrangement like this can be improved upon by making up a piece of sennit. I have a dressing gown belt, made during the 2nd World War, that is cotton string made up as 8-strand square sennit (page 26) with the ends finished as tassels and dyed, perhaps, in permanent blue ink.

A far more advanced belt can be made using Portuguese sennit, or square knotting, one of the main ingredients for all macramé. Belts like this were a favorite item for sailors to make; fine fancy ones in color for a girl at home, white ones to be traded with an officer for a favor, or just for their own use. I will give you the essentials of a plain and simple belt, how to start and finish, with plain square knotting in between. For further decoration use color, or variations of knots that can be found in *The Ashley Book of Knots* or macramé books.

Materials

A belt buckle of your choice

Some fine line preferably quite hard laid, 1/16" diam

It is difficult to specify how many lengths of material will be needed as this will depend on the width of the buckle and how many square knots can be tied side by side to make that width. This must be worked out by making up a small sample piece

The length of the individual pieces of line will depend on the length of the belt. When square knotting you need the lengths to be 4-5 times the finished length. As we start at the point of the belt with the line doubled back, the actual pieces of line will be about 9 times the finished belt length. To make a belt approximately 4 feet long you will need to cut your line in 33-40 foot lengths

Knots used

Portuguese sennit/square knotting: see also page 19

Method

I always start at the shaped end of the belt and finish at the buckle, as it is so much easier to hide the ends behind the buckle and the pointed end is the part that is handled the most, so needs to be strong and neat. For the start it helps to have some pins and a piece of soft board, such as

insulating board, a thick cork tile, a piece of soft foam covered with cloth, or even a cushion or pillow, but it is possible to work it in your hands. Start by middling 2 pieces of line, folding them back on themselves. Make the first piece of Portuguese sennit or square knotting by tying the outer 2 strands around

a

The shaped end start shown open for clarity but all knots should be pulled up snug

the middle 2 strands. Then place 2 more middled pieces of line either side of your first square knot and with 2 of the ends from the first knot and 2 new ends make another square knot, first one side of the initial knot and repeat the other, so making new square knots either side of the first (see illustration). Carry on linking the square knots and adding in extra pairs of line until the required width is reached. You can now keep up the square knotting for the entire length of the belt. Make sure that each row is the same, and that you make every square knot the same way. When you reach the buckle, bring the ends around the bar of the buckle and tie them off with a square knot around themselves with the ends at the back of the belt buckle, tucked back, parallel

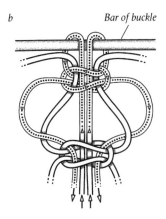

b   *Bar of buckle*

The finish at the buckle from the back, shown open for clarity but all knots should be pulled up snug

with the core strands of the last couple of pieces of the Portuguese sennit. For some materials you may feel that a little touch of glue will help to hold any loose ends in place.

A Jib Shackle

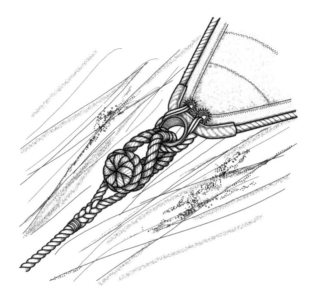

When crawling around on the foredeck with the jib flapping around your head, the last thing you want is a lump of metal trying to hit you as well. How the jib sheets are fixed to the jib is quite important. This rope jib shackle is a safe substitute for the metal shackle so often used. I call it a Dutchman's jib shackle because that is what James Lawrence, the Brightlingsea sailmaker, called it when I first spotted this useful arrangement of lanyard knot, double crown, and seizing.

We get many a Dutch visitor to the east coast of England and I guess it was first introduced to our region by one such visitor. There are other variations using the boatswain's whistle lanyard knot (page 17) but this version of the lanyard knot, based on a wall knot with a double crown finish, gives a good wide flat button. This lanyard knot was used as the stopper knot on the lanyard that is reeved through the deadeyes to set up standing rigging.

Materials

3½ feet of ⅜" 3-strand rope
A few meters of whipping twine

Knots used

Lanyard knot: diagram a
Double crown: see page 24
Flat seizing: see page 29

Method

Middle the rope and put on a flat seizing about 8¾" from the bight. Unlay the ends and make a wall knot with the 6 strands making the extra tuck as shown in the illustration. Carefully work fairly tight, but not too tight, as the ends now have to be crowned and tucked down the middle in the same way we finish the star knot (page 24), making a double crown knot. If you have a hot knife or even a heated hacksaw blade, trim the ends close to the back of the knot. Now make another flat seizing to make a loop just big enough to allow the knot to be "buttoned" through. You can now use this instead of that wicked metal shackle.

The finished jib shackle

a

Tuck all strands as shown

The Ocean & Prolong Mats

Rope mats are very satisfying to make, be they small for a glass to sit on, bigger to go under a plate, or bigger still to wipe shoes on before coming on to a boat or into a house. Door mats are a useful way of using worn-out sheets or halyards or even lifeboat falls. Be warned that mats use a lot more rope than you would expect. It is worth keeping a note of the amount of rope that has gone into a particular mat, for later reference.

The ocean and prolong mats are the most common of rope mats and are both constructed in the same manner; the only difference is that one starts from an overhand knot and the other from a carrick bend. The overhand knot start gives a mat with 3 bights on its side, while the carrick bend start gives a mat with 4 bights to the side. In both cases, they can be lengthened by repeating the basic twist and tuck process used to start them—each time this is done the mat gets another 3 bights to its side. As with all flat knot mats, you make the initial knot and then follow around to double, triple, quadruple, or even go as many as 6 times around. If, when you have made your mat you find it a bit on the small side, then it is possible to increase the whole by coiling rope round the outside of the mat and sewing the turns together.

Materials

26" x 16" ocean mat 4 times around uses 82½ feet of ½" rope
24" x 14" ocean mat 3 times around uses 46 feet of ¾" rope
32" x 16" prolong mat 4 times around uses 100 feet of ½" rope
40" x 18" prolong mat 4 times around uses 96 feet of 1" rope

Knots used

Ocean mat: diagrams a,b and c
Carrick bend style start: diagram d
Side splice finish: page 91, 92
or flat seizing: page 29

Method

In the middle of the rope, tie either an overhand knot (diagram **a**) or a carrick bend (diagram **d**) with the ends on the same side (sometimes called the

a

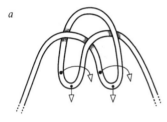

Josephine knot). Pull down a pair of loops and twist and overlay as in diagram **b**, then bring down first one end of the rope and then the other, interweaving to complete the design. The knot can

then be followed around in both directions as many times as you like or as the rope allows. When you've got the mat to the rough size and shape, it is then time to work any slack or irregularity out; do this a bit at a time as it is very difficult to work slack back into a mat that has become too tight.

c

Now follow around as many times as required

d

From this start the prolong mat can be made in the same way as the ocean mat

b

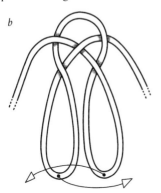

Kringle Mat

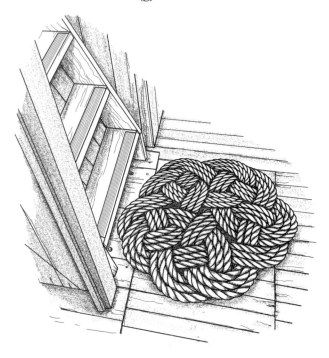

Here is a mat I first found in Kai Lund's book, *Måtter og Rosetter* (Mats and Rosettes). It consists of a series of interlinked knots that bear a similarity to the shop sign used in Denmark to denote a cake shop. This sign is in the form of the cake or biscuit called a kringle, hence the name that Kai Lund gave it. It can be tied with any number of these knots interlinked; I prefer 5, but if you want use the mat as a thump mat then 6 knots will give a slightly bigger hole in the middle to go around the eyebolt taking the block.

A mat made with 5 knots tripled in ⅛" line makes an ideal mat for a coffee cup; the same mat in ¼" would be ideal for the teapot to stand on, while if you made one in ⅜" or ½" rope and followed around 5 times you would have a useful mat for the bottom of the companionway steps, giving a modest yacht a touch of class. By making a long series of interlinked knots and opening out the center, the whole resulting knot can be arranged as an alternative to a Turk's head to decorate a tiller or such like.

Materials

13 feet of ⅛" cord will make a 5-knot mat followed around 3 times of about 4" in diam

18 feet of ¼" rope will make a 5-knot mat 3 times around of about 7¼" diam

122 feet of ⅜" rope will make a 5-knot mat followed around 5 times of about 24" in diam

Knots used

Kringle mat: diagrams a and b
Flat seizing: page 29
or side splice finish: page 91, 92

Method

Starting somewhere near the middle of the rope make the initial knot form. You may wish to pin the cord in place, but I find I can hold it in position with the flat of my hand. Bring the rope around and make the second knot, interlinking it with the first. Carry on until you get to the fifth knot, which should interlink to complete the circle. Make the knots even and neat and follow around first, with one end of the rope and then in the other direction with the other end.

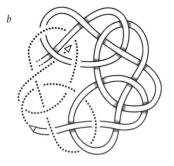

b

Follow round as many times as required

When the required number of passes have been made, the mat should be worked to a neat and even form, working out any slack a bit at a time. It is much easier to work slack out of a loose mat than it is to work a bit of slack back into a tight mat. You may find that a gentle thump with a mallet will help to flatten and even out the mat. When your mat is how you wish it to be, finish the ends off at the back either by side splicing (page 91, 92) or seizing (page 29).

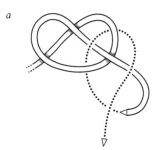

a

Oblong Deck Mat

If you have the time and the material this makes a very fine mat to collect any shoreside dirt before visitors board your boat. At home it makes a handsome door mat that will give years of use. I find that ⅜" rope gives a good balance between cost, size, and time in making, but do use whatever material you can lay your hands on. If the rope is 3 stranded it is possible to make a very neat mat side splice that is almost invisible after a little use and will allow you to turn the mat over to even out the wear. Tied in ¼", you can make a place mat for the galley table.

Materials

A mat with 5 passes: about 28" x 18", needs 150 feet of ⅜" (preferably 3 strand) rope

A mat with 5 passes: about 10" x 6½", needs 56 feet of ¼" rope

Knots used

Oblong mat: diagrams a and b
Side splice finish: diagrams c and d
or flat seizing: page 29

Method

Divide your rope into 2 equal
parts, neatly hanking each half.
With one hank or bundle, lay out
the design on the floor, if it is
doormat sized, or on a table if it
is to be a table mat. You will need

a

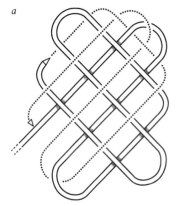

has been tied, follow round until
the rope runs out, then tighten
the mat up a little. It is not easy

b

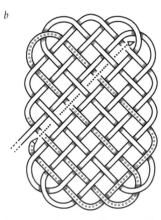

Follow round as many times as required

c

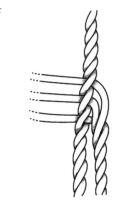

to keep a close eye on the various
overs and unders as they do not
follow any logical pattern until
the final pass that will lock the
whole design. This initial
layout should be a lot bigger
than the finished size so that
you may pass a whole bundle of
line over and under rather than
pulling the best part of 66 feet of
rope as a single length through
each time. After the initial knot

Start of the side splice

to keep the design even at this stage, as the rope goes first inside then outside as it follows the path around the mat. Keep on working the mat into shape and following around with the slack that you build up. When you have gone around 5 times, you can work any slack or deformity out and finish off with the mat side splice if using 3-strand rope or seize (see page 29) the 2 ends. Do make sure that the mat is laid out correctly, good and fair before being put to use. If one of the strands is out of place and repeatedly trodden down it is very difficult to correct later.

d

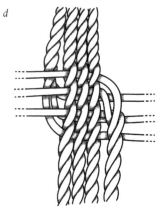

The complete side splice finish to the mat; work tight

Appendix

Useful suppliers of cordage

West Marine
Website store locator:
www.westmarine.geoserve.com/
forms/WestMarine.asp

Martin Combs
E-mail: roundturn@hotmail.com
Website: www.knotstuff.com

The Knot Shoppe
PO Box-202607
Anchorage,-
Alaska-99520-2607
USA
Tel: 00 1 (907) 274-2321
E-mail:-
knot_tyer@knotical-arts.com
Website: www.knotical-arts.
com/

R&W Enterprises
404 Nash Road,
PO Box 50420
New Bedford, MA 02746,
USA
Tel: 00 1 508/997-3933
Fax: 00 1 508/997-9990
Email: rope@randwenterprises.
com
Website: www.rwrope.com

Further reading

For me books have always been a great source of knowledge and inspiration.

This is not a full bibliography of knot books, but a selection of books that I think will help to expand on various areas of knotting and so increase your versatility.

C W Ashley, *The Ashley Book of Knots*
G Budworth, *The Hamlyn Book of Knots: Ornamental and Useful*
C Day, *The Art of Knotting and Splicing*
R Edwards, *Knots Useful and Ornamental*
R Edwards, *Turk's Heads*
S Grainger, *Creative Ropecraft*
S Grainger, *Knotcraft*
R Graumont & J Hensel, *The Encyclopaedia of Knots and Fancy Ropework*
P P O Harrison, *The Harrison Book of Knots*
F Hin, *The Colour Book of Knots*
C Jones, *The Fender Book*
Knotting Matters, the magazine of the International Guild of
    Knot Tyers
L Popple, *Advanced Ropeworking*
D Pawson, *The Handbook of Knots*
D Pawson, *The Pocket Guide to Knots and Splices*
H G Smith, *The Marlinespike Sailor*
B Toss, *The Rigging Handbook*
Q Winch, *Nets and Knots*

The International Guild of Knot Tyers

The International Guild of Knot Tyers was founded in 1982. It is a registered charity with the declared object of 'the advancement of education by the study of the art, craft and science of knotting, past and present'. The Guild regularly publishes a magazine, *Knotting Matters*, that is sent to all members. There are now well over 1250 members in over 25 countries. Groups of members meet together both in small local meetings and much larger international meetings. Membership is open to all who have an interest in knot tying, be they highly skilled or just beginners.

For more information please contact:

The Honorary Secretary
Nigel Harding
16 Egles Grove
Uckfield
East Sussex, TN22 2BY
England

Or you can check out the International Guild of Knot Tyers website www.igkt.net

Ann Norman is both a professional rope maker and an illustrator, with a lengthy interest in knots, weaving and ply-splitting (a newly-researched technique, deceptively described as 'poking ropes through ropes'). She is a member of the International Guild of Knot Tyers.

Included in her illustration and graphic design work are major books on ply-splitting and braiding. She has also published her own book on the Tibetan Twister, a four-strand cord-maker she helped adapt from a device for spinning yak hair used by Tibetan nomads. With her husband, she has co-published books on ply-splitting and weaving and is currently collaborating on a ply-splitting book for beginners.

Ann would like to thank Dauntsey's School in-Wiltshire for the many details within-the illustrations of their tall ship *Jolie Brise*, the overall winner of the Tall Ships 2000 Race and three times winner of the Fastnet Race.

Index